Transpersonal approaches to counseling and psychotherapy

Gay Hendricks
Barry Weinhold
University of Colorado - Colorado Springs

LOVE PUBLISHING COMPANY
Denver · London

Contents

Contents

Introduction

We live in an expanding universe. This notion, observed by Einstein and his followers, can tell us much about life and how it works. Life is expansion, although sub-themes of contraction certainly occur within the larger context of expansion. Therapists need only help people open up to the growth processes already unfolding within them.

Our galaxy, the cosmic neighborhood in which we live, is shaped like a spiral. This, too, can tell us much about counseling and life. A spiral reaches up and out from a center into the unknown. What the center might be, and where the spiral may be going, are key questions to consider in formulating a transpersonal approach to counseling and psychotherapy.

The book you are holding has been written as a spiral within a context of expansion. It begins with a statement of some basic ideas that seem central to a transpersonal approach, then spirals out into such areas as feelings, body and mind, relationships, child development, movement, and philosophy. What is most practical in the book is also permeated with theory, and what is most theoretical can be readily put into practice.

Both of the authors came to a transpersonal approach after many years of training and practice in analytic, humanistic, and behavioral approaches. The quest that brought us here had one driving motive: to find what works. Therefore, nothing appears in this book because it sounds good or is theoretically solid. Although we refer to the ideas of others, the book is founded on our own personal experiences and on our evolution as therapists. We use the first person because we discovered what we know through personal experience. You will find what is true only when you confirm it for yourself. We have signed each chapter so you can tell to whom the *I* in that chapter belongs. At the end of chapter 2 we have included a dialogue between us regarding our individual perspectives.

Writing this book was a discovery process for us. We invite you to become part of this process, too. Your evolution will continue, as will ours. And since we live in a spiral galaxy, in an expanding universe, we celebrate the unfinished and hope that these ideas and practices will be regarded by you as experiments that will ultimately be verified only by your own experience.

G. H.

B. W.

1

An Overview

Gay Hendricks

In the past two decades we have seen the emergence of a robust new force in psychology — the transpersonal approach. Transpersonal psychology, with striking implications for all fields of human endeavor, most directly impacts education and the helping professions. Counseling and psychotherapy are often the natural proving ground for any new approach, and transpersonal psychology — sometimes called the Fourth Force because it followed the Freudian, behavioral, and humanistic movements — must be carefully examined to determine if it can contribute something of new and lasting value to our understanding of personality and its transformation.

DEFINING THE INDEFINABLE

Anthony Sutich, one of the founders (with Abraham Maslow) of both the Association for Humanistic Psychology and later the Association for Transpersonal Psychology, once said that *transpersonal* was indefinable and should remain so. He was concerned with the tendency of definitions to limit a phenomenon and believed that transpersonal psychology, of all things, must not be limited. Nevertheless, it may be possible to suggest several broad definitions that, when considered in their essences, communicate the scope of the field without placing limiting boundaries upon it.

The Latin prefix *trans* has several meanings. It can mean *connecting*, in the sense of a transatlantic telephone cable. It can also mean *through*, in the sense of a transparent pane of glass. A third meaning is *beyond*, as in the word transcendental. Adding these three meanings of *trans* to the word *personal*, we have a term that refers to bridging and connecting the personal, through the personal, and beyond the personal. What can this be? What is it that connects all persons, is at the essence of all persons, and is beyond the purely personal? To answer these questions, let us explore the Latin root of *personal*. In Latin, the term *persona* means mask. A *persona* is a mask that one dons for a certain purpose. An example of the use of this term in English is our word denoting personality, which is based upon *persona*. Personality can be understood as a set of masks we don to gain recognition and approval, or to protect ourselves from pain. Assemble a variety of *personas*, or masks, and you have a personality. Transpersonal can therefore refer to that which is through the *persona*, beyond the *persona*, connecting all *personas*.

Much of Western psychology can be regarded as ego psychology, because it deals with processes of the *personal*ity by which we seek recognition and protect ourselves from pain. The term *ego* comes from a word that means *I*. Thus, the *I* of most Western psychology refers to ego. Grof, in his important book *Realms of the Human Unconscious*, defined transpersonal experiences as those that go beyond the normal boundaries of the ego.[1]

---

1. Stanislav Grof, *Realms of the Human Unconscious* (New York: Viking Press, 1974).

The ego, then — the central focus of study for much of the psychology of the West — is but the jumping-off place for transpersonal psychology.

What remains after the masks of *persona* have been removed? What is beyond the strivings of the ego? What aspects of human experience go beyond and through the personal while connecting all persons?

Abraham Maslow, known for positing a hierarchy of human needs, was one of the founders of transpersonal psychology. Frequently depicted in the form of a pyramid, the hierarchy arrayed human needs as follows:

The middle three sets of needs, including safety/security, love/belonging, and self-esteem, can be regarded as ego needs because they involve acquiring and maintaining a set of successful *personas* with which to get one's needs met. Maslow's "highest need" was self-actualization, the emergence of one's true self in some form of creative expression. By higher, he did not mean better. Just as the higher rungs of a ladder are no better than the lower, the higher human needs were so placed because they depend upon successfully meeting the lower, more basic needs.

In the final version of the hierarchy, published toward the end of Maslow's life, he made a revealing addition. At the top of the pyramid, beyond self-actualization, Maslow placed a need for transcendence. A modified version of the pyramid might look like this:

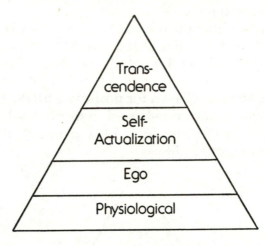

Transcendence, or surrender into an expanded sense of self, is the need that grows out of self-actualization. The higher needs are likely present in a subtle form throughout our development, but must await the successful meeting of more basic needs before they can be acknowledged. Before the ego needs can be met, breakfast must be served. Before self-actualization can get under way, we must have a workable sense of self. Then, with a full stomach, an effective ego, and an emerging relationship with our true and creative self, we can set about the task of dissolving our personal conception of ourselves and begin to surrender to the transpersonal.

A TRANSPERSONAL CONTEXT

As part of the transpersonal approach, counselors incorporate a set of activities and processes designed to change thoughts, feelings, and behaviors. A counselor may meditate with a client, for example, or may use intuition to tune in to some aspect of a client's life. But basic to determining whether or not the counselor is working from a transpersonal approach are his or her attitudes and views. Some attitudes that many transpersonal therapists would agree are part of a transpersonal context are discussed in the following pages.

Oneness

The ego, by its very nature, is a seeker. It restlessly scans the environment in search of recognition. It tirelessly protects against threats to itself. It is on the make, on the run. It sees separateness; that is its job. But a transpersonal therapist knows that the ego is only part of the picture. The ego has been compared to being like the mayor of New York City — important, yes, but to be kept in perspective.

Mystics throughout the millenia have emerged from their meditations with a simple, profound truth that has life-changing implications: We are one. They mean that we are one both within ourselves and without.

Most psychological problems can be viewed as stemming from forgetting that we are all one. For example, it is not our emotions per se that cause so much difficulty; rather, it is our attempts to disown our emotions. We may have a feeling like anger that would soon dissolve if we acknowledged, accepted, and expressed it. If, however, we do not accept it or express it, we tie up energy in suppressing it. If this tendency to hold emotions at arm's length, instead of embracing them, becomes a lifestyle, we have a problem that is likely to affect our relationship with ourselves and with others. Conversely, knowing that we are all one can help us befriend the disowned parts of ourselves — thus allowing us to develop a sense of unity.

Problems in relationships between people have the same root as do psychological or emotional problems. When we forget that we are one with all other humans, when we regard each other as separate ego entities, we tend to misunderstand others and feel alienated.

A transpersonal world view, which transcends ego boundaries, sees all parts as being equal in the whole, all humans as having the same needs, feelings, and potentials.

An Expansionist View ————————————————————————

Transpersonal approaches tend to be expansionist rather than reductionist in their view of the human personality and potential. The transpersonal, as the Fourth Force in psychology, has built upon contributions of the first three forces — Freudian, behavioral, and humanistic. Whereas an approach like classic behaviorism tends to be reductionistic, in reducing large sets of phenomena to fit smaller sets of processes (reinforcement, stimulus, response), transpersonal approaches tend to be open-ended and inclusive. So, although a behaviorist (for example) might not acknowledge transpersonal phenomena, a transpersonalist would almost certainly acknowledge behavioral phenomena like reinforcement and conditioning.

Transpersonal approaches draw upon the first three forces while going beyond to see humans as intuitive, mystical, psychic, and spiritual. Above all, humans are viewed as unifiable, having the potential for harmonious and holistic development of all their potentials.

Acceptance and Use of the Full Human Potential ————————

One of the hallmarks of the transpersonal approach is the acceptance and use of the farther reaches of human potential. Among the extraordinary phenomena that the transpersonal therapist acknowledges and puts to use are altered states of consciousness, mystical insight, paranormal powers, and the human quest for unity and contact with the divine.

The use of altered states of consciousness in counseling might take several forms. Transpersonal counselors may use relaxation training, guided fantasy, or meditation to accomplish various goals in counseling. Relaxation training, for example, has proven to be useful in dealing with common problems like test anxiety, in addition to more serious problems like agoraphobia and anorexia nervosa. Furthermore, relaxation, centering, and other such skills can be taught to students in school as a preventive mental hygiene tool, regardless of whether or not a problem exists.

The concept of altered states of consciousness has another fundamental application in counseling. It communicates to the client that valid alternatives to ordinary, linear, waking consciousness are available. In Western culture the linear, logical approach to solving problems is highly valued. This is the state of consciousness that builds bridges, conducts experiments, smashes atoms. But life presents other problems, emotional difficulties, communication blocks, crises that are not easily handled through the rational approach. Actually, many problems may be *caused* by an overly rational approach to life. I recall a session with an engineer and his wife in which he was being confronted because he was unable to hear and respond to his wife's feelings. "Feelings?" he asked in puzzlement. "I've worked my whole career at getting the human error out of situations, and now you want me to listen to somebody's *feelings?*"

Nonrational processes like dreaming and meditation can indeed yield material relevant to therapy, material that may have been elusive in ordinary working consciousness. To give an example, I once worked with a person who was trying to make a decision about taking a new job. The change had many implications, and this client had worried over it for several months without being able to come to a decision. I suggested to him that his logical processes had probably considered the issue from every angle, and perhaps it was time to find out what the innermost part of him had to say about it. I asked him to pay attention to his dreams for a couple of nights to see if they would yield any useful information. That night he dreamed of crossing a large body of water. The journey was fraught with difficulty, but as he reached the shore on the other side, he saw a traffic light. It was green. He felt on awaking that he had received the go-ahead from the deeper part of himself, and he took the new job. Now, after several successful years, he feels that it was the right move for him at the time.

Along with altered states of consciousness, the transpersonal approach takes into account the insights received from mystical and psychic experiences. Though other approaches might see these processes as irrelevant or even pathological, the transpersonal approach makes room for and even celebrates explorations into the farther reaches of human potential.

There is no question, for anyone who reads the literature in the field, that events such as telepathy and precognition do take place. How they work is not known, since psychic processes do not readily lend themselves to scientific investigation. One of the aims of the transpersonal approach is to regard psychic processes as normal rather than paranormal. Not enough is known about these processes to determine just how they may best be used in therapy. Nevertheless, we can make space for psychic events in our conceptual framework so that we can be open to their occurrence. We can take on a willing attitude of inquiry toward them. Then they may surprise us by how they work.

In recent years I have been experiencing more and more seemingly telepathic contact when working with clients. In the first session of working with one couple, I had an impulse to tell the wife to give the husband more latitude and leeway regarding a particular issue. The specific thought entering my mind was, "Get off his back." I kept silent, as I was not sure I had good enough rapport with the wife to confront her this directly. The next week she came in and very excitedly told me that the problem had cleared up in a particularly unusual way. When I asked her how this had happened, she replied that several hours after our first session she had suddenly realized, "I need to get off Carl's back." Coincidence could be a useful explanation in one or two events like this, but after accumulating a sizeable number of them, I now find telepathy to be a sounder explanation.

Spiritual Dimensions

The transpersonal view also acknowledges the human spiritual quest. Transpersonal therapists accept the human need for growth along spiritual dimensions such as unity, ultimate truth, and direct perception of the divine. Humans are seen as ultimately spiritual in addition to physical, emotional, and mental.

Namaste

A traditional Indian greeting, *namaste,* can be translated as, "I salute the light within you." This term captures an important attitude that transpersonal therapists can transmit to clients. There is a light within us all. Counselors often see people who have lost perspective; they have become identified with their problems. It can be a true revelation for them to learn that while they may *have* problems, they are more than their problems. We can perceive a part within us that is essence, free of all the conditioned elements of the personality. Whether this is termed a soul, a spirit, or a self, it is the timeless part of all of us that is beyond conditioning.

We might think of ourselves as a lantern with a light shining brightly within. Life experiences, parental conditioning, societal pressure, and other factors put smudges on the chimney of the lantern, making the light less perceptible to ourselves and others. Working on ourselves through counseling, meditation, or other practices can polish the chimney so the light can shine through.

Transpersonal therapists have trained themselves to see the light in themselves and others, even when it is buried beneath a lifetime of smudge.

Wisdom is Beyond Belief

Psychological growth depends upon the transcendence or erasing of a person's history of conditioned thoughts, feelings, and behavior. Georges Gurdjieff proffered that humans were asleep, mechanically responding in a conditioned manner. Awakening could come only through self-observation and "work on oneself" through mental and physical discipline. The Indian teacher Krishnamurti once remarked that the word *guru* was widely misunderstood to connote a person who dispensed some sort of knowledge, whereas the true and original meaning of the term meant a person who *dispelled* knowledge. The guru's task is to help seekers cut through the knowledge they have about the world and themselves and, by doing so, to tap into the creative source of knowledge that is beyond their conditioned purview.

What we know about our world is often what someone else has trained us to think and believe about it. The task of growth is not to learn something else, but to erase the distorted knowledge we already have so we can see the world inside and outside afresh.

Karma

The concept of *karma* figures largely in Asian spiritual systems. Although karma, particularly in the Hindu system, is used to imply the transfer of destiny from one lifetime to another, a more personal, here-and-now understanding of the term can be useful with clients. Karma, in our understanding, refers to the unconscious patterns of behavior that we have learned from adults who taught us. Unless one becomes conscious of these patterns and changes them, they can go on unabated from one generation to another and appear to be predetermined.

Another way of understanding karma is to see it as an opportunity to embrace what we have in the past repelled. We may have within us the fear of being alone, for example. But by withdrawing from this fear, we propel ourselves into situations that call forth the fear. Thus, in trying to withdraw from an experience, we create a destiny in which we are forced to confront that experience.

As an application of this concept, say we have an aversion to someone. We may turn away to avoid confronting the person or our own feelings about the person, but we curiously find that the person pops up everywhere in our lives, either in person or in our minds. Until we act to *embrace* our own reactions and the actual person, we reinforce our reactions rather than changing them. If we view the experience through an understanding of karma, we will create a destiny full of opportunities for embracing it. We must, in truth, forgive that person and what he or she represents in ourselves before we can embrace the perfection of the universe as it operates through us.

Understanding the concept of karma gives us an entirely different way to look at our lives. Viewing life as a series of opportunities rather than obstacles is in itself a radical change in consciousness.

Observation and Love

Observation — seeing things the way they are — is a key part of many systems of psychological and spiritual growth. Observation means the ability to see thoughts, feelings, and behavior as they are with no evaluation. It is original meeting original without anything in between. When we observe things as they are, without judgment, they begin to change. This is because we have added awareness to the equation, and awareness is not just one of the powers that make us fully human; it is an agent of change. Then, when we can learn to *love* things as they are, they are no longer that way! When we learn to love our fear or our anger, we replace the feeling with acceptance. When we learn to love a previously hated body, we transform the energy that was trapped in hatred. Thus liberated, the energy can be used for change.

This is why it works: Most of us waste energy in resisting, in setting up a duality between what is and what we want it to be. Here we refer primarily to what is within us — our fear, anger, sexual feelings, all the things we usually dislike ourselves for having. To accept and love others is difficult until we do the same for ourselves. We continue to resist *what is,* though — often in the name of self-improvement. Tremendous energy is required to maintain a stance of resistance, particularly since the feelings, thoughts, and behaviors we most resist seem to be those that recycle most frequently. Paradoxically, then, the only ultimately successful way to change is by lovingly accepting all parts of us, just as we are.

The Sufi poet Rumi once wrote, "The astrolabe of God's mysteries is love." The astrolabe was a navigational device for finding one's way around the stars. So Rumi was saying that love is the tool for navigating through the mysteries of ourselves.

Love may be the only part of us that needs awakening; once we know how to love ourselves and all our reactions to things, we have the tools needed to explore our psychodynamic and spiritual potentials.

Here are some questions about love that clients have asked, along with the answers to them:

Q: Is loving ourselves the same as egotism?

A: No, egotism is an attempt to convince the world and ourselves that we are lovable after we have come to hate ourselves.

Q: What can we do if we can't love ourselves?

A: We can love ourselves for not being able to love ourselves.

Q: If we love ourselves for all our anger, sexuality, and violence, won't we go around being angry, violent, and incontinent?

A: No, we act out anger and other feelings inappropriately because we resist them until they explode. If we lovingly accept all our feelings, they can be channeled into appropriate expression.

Other Transpersonal Attitudes

A commonly held transpersonal attitude is that the way out is *through*. The only way to quit feeling scared, or angry, or sad is to go ahead and give ourselves total permission to feel that way, if only for a moment. For example, a young girl had experienced some problems in relating to boys, and her counselor suspected that she was still angry at her father for some things he did and didn't do when she was younger. The counselor encouraged her to express the anger, and when she had, the counselor asked her to love herself for feeling angry. Afterward, she realized that she did not have to be attached to that anger any more, that she could let it go. A smile spread over her face, and she looked transformed. She had opened up, accepted her anger, expressed it, and let it go. In the process her consciousness expanded to embrace something that before was resisted and contained.

In summary, we may say that transpersonal approaches take a broader view of humans than do most approaches to therapy. Transpersonal counseling, like other therapies, sees people as hindered by psychodynamic conflicts, but the transpersonal orientation takes into account the human impulse toward higher states of consciousness. Transpersonal therapists also may draw from spiritual systems in addition to psychological systems for explaining phenomena in the therapeutic quest. And they may use techniques (e.g., meditation, energy awareness, imagery, relaxation, love) that tend to go beyond those used by traditional therapists.

THE CORE NATURE OF HUMANS

The core of the human personality, according to the transpersonal view, is not ego. Transpersonal definitions of ego place it among the components of human personality. The core is really where all life energy resides and where our connection with universal energy begins. This core, along with those dynamic processes that tend to obscure the core, can be illustrated by an open circle and five expanding circles around it.

The Core

We have within us something that is essence, free from the residue accumulated by conditioning and the unfinished business of living. A metaphor for this open space could be a window through which others can see the inner light of ourselves, and through which we can receive the world the way it is, without distortion. When all the screens have been removed from the window and it has been lovingly polished, a new set of possibilities opens for us.

This human core might be regarded as the most basic of the transpersonal common denominators. While most of us have come to think of a common denominator as the lowest level at which two or more entities come together, here is a paradox: The core at once unifies all humans on the *highest* level — the level at which, free from the conditioned differences in feeling, thought, perception, and behavior, we are all the same, and one.

15

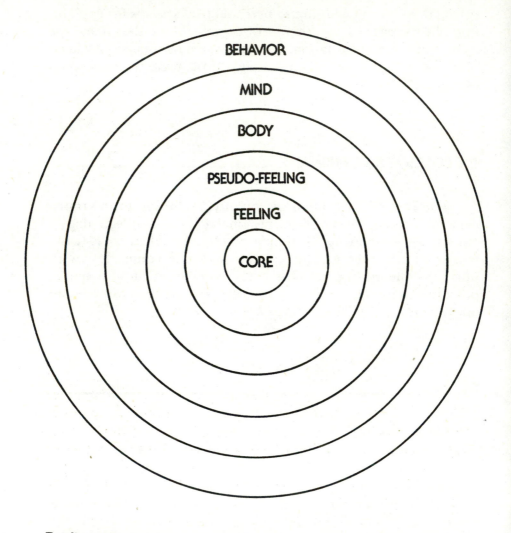

Feeling

Early in life a second circle is placed over the open space. Although quite translucent, it is the beginning of a process of distortion. This circle is emotion, feeling.

Feeling does not severely distort the essence. The basic feelings are only a few: fear, anger, sadness, happiness, excitement. When we do not resist them, when we experience them fully, we have access to the core. Thus, our feelings are one of the most direct avenues to the spiritual essence within. Were we to be in contact

with our most basic feelings on a daily basis, we would be living very close to the core. But a more serious distortion occurs as parental and societal conditioning begins. We might call this layer of distortion pseudo-feelings.

Pseudo-Feelings

We use pseudo-feelings to defend ourselves against the basic feelings beneath. An example of this is the learned use of anger when the real feeling beneath is fear. Those who have not been given permission to feel or express fear often turn it into anger, which may get the attention of the people around them. Other people cover deep anger with fear; they are, in essence, scared of their anger. The pseudo-feelings are a troubling distortion because they seem like real feelings, but are instead among the most

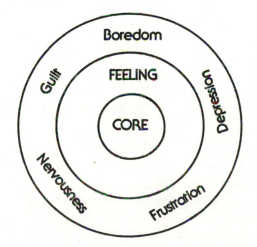

difficult to penetrate of all the layers of defense against the basic feelings. Pseudo-feelings include blame, guilt, shame, depression, frustration, nervousness, irritation, and boredom.

The Body

This circle is denser and more material. It is the physical, bodily layer of defense, some examples of which are:

- muscular tension (unnecessary contraction of skeletal muscles)
- postural attitude (examples: head forward, shoulders hunched, locked knees, stomach sucked in, tensed brow)
- postural imbalance (weight carried unevenly front to back or side to side)
- autonomic hyperarousal (fast heartbeat, excessive sweat production, rapid respiration)
- psychosomatic illness (asthmas, rashes, ulcers, colitis).

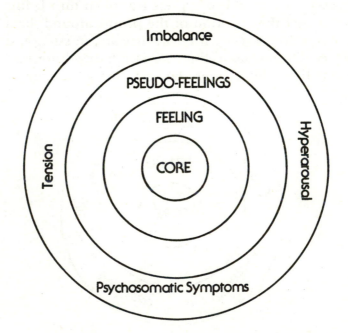

Excess muscle tension, a common example, causes a number of problems. First, muscle tension warps the body and pulls it out of alignment with gravity. Second, tension is associated with many psychosomatic symptoms, from headaches, many of which are caused by tension in the muscles on the back of the head and neck, to high blood pressure, in which the flow of blood is restricted by the surrounding tense musculature. Third, tense muscles constitute a barrier to feeling. The rigid muscles act as a wall of defense against the feelings trapped inside, and against the feelings of others.

Mental Layer _____

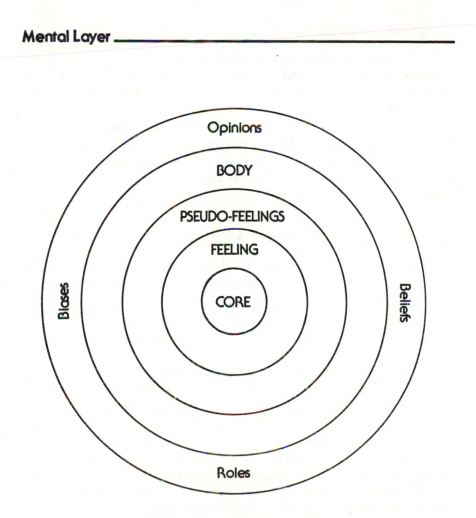

In proceeding from the inner layers of defense to the outer, the distortions become more complex, and now we come to a defense system so infinitely complex that few ever get beneath it. This is the mental layer of distortion, containing all our beliefs, biases, prejudices, perceptions, and conditioned ways of thinking.

Of course, not all mental activity is problematic. We can use mental mechanisms to handle information and solve problems. But if we observe ourselves closely, we can see that much of our mental activity is unproductive and uninvited, and it distorts our ability to see things clearly.

Behaviors

The outermost layer of distortion and defense consists of all our observable verbal and nonverbal behaviors. These include the way we talk, the roles we occupy, our gestures, and all the "games people play."

Not all of these behaviors are problematic either. People can solve problems, communicate effectively, enjoy intimacy, and take on meaningful roles. Nevertheless, few of us feel satisfied with our ability to do these things with satisfactory frequency or consistency. Most of us present to the world a limited repertoire of conditioned verbal and nonverbal behaviors. And the conditioned patterns of acting and speaking perpetuate our problems rather than solve them.

To illustrate the various levels of reality represented by the circles, let us use an example of a set of twins. At the core, Joe and Jill simply *are*. They are essence, pure being, uncolored and unsullied by any concept, notion, or conditioning that can be applied to them. At this deepest level, they are simply representatives of life energy.

At the feeling level, some differences between the two begin to emerge. Although both Joe and Jill have all the feelings common to humans, Joe gets angry more often than Jill. She, on the other hand, becomes afraid more often. At the level of pseudo-feelings, their differences emerge more clearly. Joe deals with his anger by pouting, sulking and getting depressed. Jill deals with her fear by being nervous. Joe's shoulders are tense and held back, and a shoulder massage hurts him. Jill has relaxed shoulder muscles, but she has a tight stomach, accompanied by frequent stomach upsets.

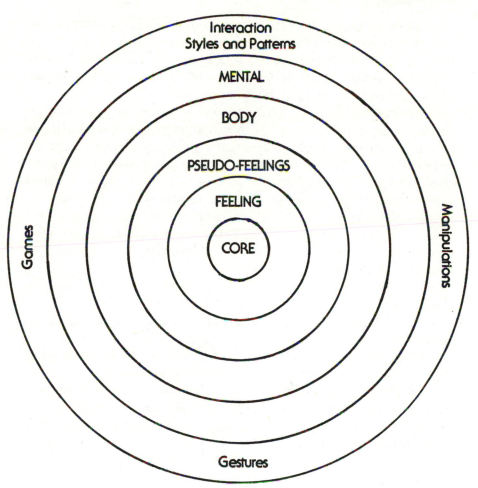

Jill is highly critical of herself in her mind. If criticized, she automatically thinks she is in the wrong. Joe, in contrast, thinks that he is right and others are wrong. If criticized, he is likely to be defiant and start an argument.

As you can see, the farther we get from the core, the more complex the phenomena become. At the core, there is oneness. At the levels of mind and behavior, there is infinite difference. With all the conditioned layers of feeling, thinking, and acting serving as screens, we can see why the core is obscured, why so few are in touch with the essence within. We can also see why some people who have experienced the reality of their core continue to be troubled by problems on the most external levels of themselves.

A person who experiences the core during meditation practice still has to dissolve the emotional, physical, mental, and behavioral barriers before he or she can live totally free of distortion. Dissolving these barriers takes time, awareness, and immersion in the experience of one's feeling, body, mind, and actions.

The rewards are worth it because as we begin cutting through the layers of conditioning, we begin living transpersonally; we begin dying to the old and experiencing rebirth on a moment-to-moment basis. We are propelled in this process by a powerful energy, for as we approach the core — our common connection with all life energy — we get just the amount of energy needed to dissolve the very next layer of conditioning that must be removed in order to keep growing. The choice is always ours. We may choose at any moment to withdraw our awareness or expand it to what is here and real.

IN SUMMARY

Every approach to human behavior seeks to explain what motivates us. By finding out who or what is driving us, we may learn how better to change directions. To the orthodox Freudian, sex is the driver. To the behaviorist, the search for reinforcement and the avoidance of punishment drives us. To the humanist, self-actualization is a motivating force. To all of these, the transpersonal therapist says "yes." But there's more. In the *expansive* transpersonal view, there is something in us that seeks freedom, wholeness, connection with all. There is an urge to play, to create, to go where no one has gone before. There is something beyond the strivings of the ego and the masks of the personality. It is this nameless thing that is the home ground of the transpersonal approach.

2

The Transpersonal Therapist
Barry Weinhold

The transpersonal approach to counseling and psycho-therapy includes many goals and techniques of the traditional therapies but places them in a larger, more expanded context for understanding human behavior. As part of the context, the therapist teaches clients how to expand their view of themselves, how to ground their behavior and experiences within this context, and how to assume complete responsibility for their behavior and experiences. Also, the concept of "the therapeutic experience" is enlarged to encompass all of life's experiences. The therapist teaches clients how to utilize this expanded context in their daily lives. In addition to the more conventional therapeutic techniques, the transpersonal therapist may use a variety of methods to help clients expand their awareness and reduce their attachments to more limited kinds of awarenesses.

The therapeutic process also is expanded to include a high degree of mutuality between therapist and client, in which both are working on themselves and teaching one another. Because they share a common growth-oriented intention for therapy, there is usually less distance between therapist and client than in conventional approaches. Therapy traditionally has been a process whereby one person, presumably with more experience and knowledge, tries to share his or her interpretations of that experience and knowledge with those who presumably have needs in those areas. This process inadvertently teaches people how to invalidate their own knowledge and experience in favor of someone else's. Many clients have gained an understanding of human behavior to the extent that this process now seems insulting.

We have to expand our concept of therapy to include the validation of personal experience. Inherent in this expanded view of therapy is the recognition that this form of therapy is possible every moment of the day. All the people, situations, events of our day have potential for teaching us everything we want to know about ourselves, other people, and the world around us.

> I was about to say something when John closed his eyes and took in a slow, deep breath. The air became still, and I was aware of sounds I have not heard before. I heard the bees working in the flowers bordering the veranda, the birds calling in the valley, the wind rustling the leaves, a dog barking in the distance, and the faint sound of some children playing — but it seems that I could hear them *all at once*. It was an extraordinary experience, for I realized, at that moment, that normally it only appears that we hear, or see, more than one thing at a time. Perhaps for a brief moment I knew the meaning of consciousness as a form of energy, for it was possible to realize that all the sounds were taking different lengths of time to reach my ears and thus to hear them all at once it was necessary to transcend space and time as we normally perceive it.[1]

Therapists are only the easels for displaying the experiences of life. It is these experiences, not the easels, that we wish to examine in detail. Your experience of life can teach you everything you need to know if you are but awake enough to receive the message.

---

1. Reshad Feild, *The Invisible Way: A Love Story for the New Age* (New York: Harper & Row, 1979), pp. 93-94.

All of us have had many people serving as therapists for us: mothers, fathers, professional teachers, friends, marital partners, and even our own children. Everyone you encounter is a potential therapist for you — as well as your being a potential therapist for them. Finding these therapists at first appears to be a random process, but one senses that there certainly could be some unconscious purpose behind these encounters. There is an awareness that you are dealing with more than the specifics of the moment. For example, there likely are patterns of learning for you that go beyond what we refer to as a lifetime. When you meet another person who is in that moment a therapist for you and you for him or her, there is awareness of being interwoven into one another's patterns not just in the moment, but perhaps in generations gone by and those yet to come. Time seems to have very little to do with this kind of therapy.

Who, then, are transpersonal therapists? A transpersonal therapist is anyone who chooses to be one. The main qualification is that you have made a deliberate choice to see your core self as being the same as other people's. You see that through choosing to teach others you can best teach yourself everything you need to know. Transpersonal therapy takes place when you can see someone else *as* yourself. When this focus is clear, you can see that everything you are focusing on in others is some aspect of yourself. In this context, other people bring "gifts" to you that may remind you of things you may not have accepted or understood in yourself.

DEVELOPMENT OF A TRANSPERSONAL PERSPECTIVE

Essentially, three steps are involved in developing a transpersonal perspective. The first is to become aware that all life experiences usually seen as external to oneself are actually projections of the inner self onto the screen of outer reality. The second step entails learning how to reclaim these projections. This may involve learning creative alchemy or the power to transmute the matter/energy of a problem or feeling. The third step is to finally realize that there is no difference between what is experienced as inside and what is experienced as outside. They are now seen as the same thing.

SOME BELIEFS OF TRANSPERSONAL THERAPISTS ──────

So called transpersonal therapists are those who have begun to integrate this expanded way of understanding the therapy experience. Their beliefs can be summarized as follows:

1. To do therapy is to receive therapy; the therapist and client are the same.
2. You cannot help anyone else, only yourself. Doing therapy with others is an excellent way of teaching yourself.
3. Anyone you meet is a potential therapist and client.
4. Therapy is a constant process that goes on every moment of the day and continues even into your sleep.
5. To do therapy is to demonstrate. What you demonstrate is who you are (or think you are) and what you believe your relationship to others to be.
6. The formal content of your therapy approach may be irrelevant to the way it is being given and being received.
7. Ultimately you are your own therapist. This means people must be given the tools to work with themselves.
8. Everything you see outside yourself is a projection of what is going on inside yourself. It seems easier to see it first in others or outside yourself before seeing it in yourself.
9. Thoughts are a form of energy that manifest and create your experiences.
10. It doesn't matter what therapy path you take. There are thousands of paths, and they all lead to the same place. All the answers are available to you if you are aware enough to recognize them.
11. The validity of your internal experience is to be trusted. Therefore, an internal therapist has to be someone you trust to give you information that guides and directs you in understanding your life experiences.

Let's take a closer look at each of these beliefs, described below.

To do therapy is to receive therapy. This understanding is difficult to grasp at first because it seems to run counter to most of what you are taught about therapy. Yet, it is the cornerstone of a transpersonal approach. You may have to behave "as if" this were true until you can experience the truth of the statement at a personal level. Therapy is a way of attesting to what you believe is true about yourself.

Self-therapy. This naturally grows out of the first belief and is stated separately for emphasis. If you have this focus, you certainly open up the possibility of learning more about yourself. It requires only a change in attitude but, once changed, adds a richness to all your therapy situations, whether they are formal or informal.

Everyone is your therapist and client. All people we encounter have the potential to be our therapist, our client, or both. You will attract people you need to help you solve your problems. Everyone you meet brings you a gift, even though you may not be ready to receive that gift. Your job is to determine the true nature of their gift and then learn how to utilize the gift to solve your problems. Likewise, you have gifts to offer others, who will be attracted to you for what you can bring to them.

The 24-hour therapist. This, too, expands the focus of therapy to include all of life's experiences. It really means that no matter what you are doing, the opportunities for self-improvement are always there. In all of life's experiences, you are confronted with either lessons to be learned or bliss. Once you have learned the lesson, there is more time to experience bliss.

To do therapy is to demonstrate. Richard Bach, in his fine book *Illusions*, has defined *learning* as finding out what you already know, and *teaching* as reminding others what they already know. *Doing*, according to Bach, is demonstrating what you already know. *Therapy* is a form of witnessing for yourself and others. It enables you to show yourself and others what you believe to be true.[2]

Imbedded therapy. What a therapist is saying is usually only a small part of the therapeutic effort. All the words do is get other people's attention long enough for the real therapy to occur. Your level of awareness is the true therapist and is often transmitted nonverbally or can be conveyed by the sound of your voice. These sound vibrations are actually doing the therapy no matter what you are saying at any moment.

---

2. Richard Bach, *Illusions: The Adventures of a Reluctant Messiah* (New York: Delacorte, 1977).

Self-therapy tools. If your focus has been on external rather than internal sources of information, you may need help in refocusing on them. Meditation, yoga, journal keeping, and energy awareness itself are tools that help you refocus this energy. Many of the tools mentioned in this book are readily available to all of us without much additional training.

Projection. This is the major way people invalidate themselves. It is how we keep from dealing with issues that are pressing into our awareness. Therefore, refocusing on self-energy requires a clear awareness that what you see outside yourself is *all* a projection of what is going on inside yourself. Without this awareness, you will remain hopelessly stuck in limiting your energy patterns.

Thought is creative. This belief is basic to understanding the transpersonal therapist. You have to understand that you are the source of all your thoughts and that the manifested results of your thoughts serve as therapists for you. Your results tell you clearly what your thoughts have been. If you don't like your results, you have to change your thoughts.

The myth of the single path. Many different approaches are presented as the only way to salvation. Transpersonal therapists know that this isn't true and that the path they choose is one of thousands of valid paths. In choosing a way or developing a path of your own, though, you must have some sense about the nature of that path. This includes some idea about how fast people usually are expected to move on that path (you could get trampled by going too slowly). Measure this against how fast you would like to move, and then decide a path that you can move along comfortably.

The internal therapist. You, like most of us, were taught not to listen to your internal "voices," so developing a reliable internal source may be difficult at first. One suggestion is to listen to your heart energy. The voice of your heart generally is a good source, although it may have to be balanced by some thinking. Trust that you will know by your results, if nothing else, which inner voices to listen to and which to ignore. Meditation can be useful in opening yourself to hear your internal therapist more clearly. It can cut the "noise" or chatter that your surface mind is engaging in.

SPECIAL TECHNIQUES? _____

There are no special techniques for the transpersonal therapist. The only focus is on learning the lessons imbedded in all life experiences. Therapy happens everywhere without any formal structure. There is no person or situation from whom/which a transpersonal therapist cannot learn. Likewise, there is no one he or she cannot reach. All those you meet, therefore, form a therapeutic relationship, and there is really no accident in this. If you didn't have anything to teach each other or learn from each other, you would not have met.

Some of these therapeutic situations are quite casual. Perhaps a stranger sits down next to you on an airplane. Do you talk to the person or ignore him or her? Perhaps two students in a formal class are assigned to do a project together. Do they agree or protest?

At a more sustained level (two or more people, say), a professional therapist and a group of clients may meet for a prescribed time period and then disperse. A relationship with a friend may go on for some time, and then the friend might move away. These are more intense therapeutic situations. One such situation is described below, showing how a transpersonal therapist used a temporary relationship to learn some important lessons.

"We formed a committee to help all the school staff better serve the needs of minority youngsters in our student body. We hired an expert in this field, a black fellow named Dr. Robinson. As our work with this man progressed, I realized I just didn't like the fellow. To handle these feelings of dislike, I did the usual things such as trying to see what things in him that I disliked might really be things in myself I wasn't happy with. Then I looked into what he might be doing that I wished I could get away with. I still couldn't come up with the reason I disliked him.

"Then one day it came to me. Dr. Robinson, being black, had experienced many occasions of hostility and prejudice from the white community. As could be expected, he held a lot of anger and resentment within him. In fact, that anger just seemed to fill the air with a negative energy. Although he was absolutely brilliant at disguising it with anything verbal he expressed, I could feel that anger energy and I would get uncomfortable.

"I came to the next meeting with a better understanding of what I felt about him. The meeting started out much as usual. I was sitting across the circle from Dr. Robinson and looking at him intently. Slowly the other people in the room began to fade from my consciousness and I realized all my thoughts were centered on him. It was almost as if something that had been blurred was coming into focus, and as the focus sharpened, I saw Dr. Robinson as unbelievably lonely, isolated from people of all races, even though he was at the top of his field, respected, admired. I saw him so lonely that it was hard to imagine the intensity of his loneliness, my loneliness. Then, suddenly, the loneliness just broke something within me and I loved him. It was as if the total love of the universe was flowing through me to him, surrounding him with a loving energy so intense that my whole being was vibrating with it as it flowed through me. It wasn't that I was doing anything, but rather that I was being used as a channel for this loving energy.

"I noticed a gradual change start to come over Dr. Robinson. He had laughed before — I remembered that — but it had been in a sarcastic way. I'd never seen him smile, and suddenly he was smiling in a relaxed, peaceful way. He had refused to speak about his own children. Now he was using them as examples in a warm, human way. I noticed that the other people in the room were becoming more relaxed and talking more openly than they had in any of the previous meetings. I myself was amazed by what had happened, but attributed it to my own solving of my reaction to Dr. Robinson. I didn't dare believe that this sudden flow of loving energy through me had wrought the changes I was feeling and seeing.

"It wasn't until two days later that I had reason to speak with anyone about what had happened. Then I saw one member of our committee, who remarked, 'Wasn't that some change in our meeting the other day? Dr. Robinson seemed like a *person*, a *real* person, for the first time. I felt that we really got somewhere with the meeting.' I started to shake inside. Maybe it wasn't just the way *I* was looking at things after all. Maybe the love that had been flowing through me had made a difference after all. The committee member went on to talk about the change in Dr. Robinson. He had become someone to whom she could easily relate.

"I could hardly wait to talk with other members of the committee, and as I did so I found all had noticed a difference, ranging from how changed Dr. Robinson had seemed to how much more on target the whole meeting had been. All I could do was to throw out my hands in a gesture of wonder and amazement, and to feel thankful that I had been a vehicle through which the universe poured this love energy."[3]

Finally, therapeutic situations can be imbedded in relationships that are lifelong. Marital partners, for example, are those who choose to make permanent their therapeutic relationship because they see unlimited opportunities for self-improvement. The closer a couple become to each other and their true selves, the richer the therapeutic opportunities become.

THERAPEUTIC TOOLS OR METHODS

Many therapeutic tools or methods are available to the transpersonal therapist. These are discussed in other chapters. The main tool or method of therapy available, however, is the awareness of and control over your own energy patterns. The ability to change your vibrational level and respond with the energy pattern necessary to deal with any given situation is a precise art. Many masters have studied a lifetime to learn how to develop even a small amount of control over their own vibrational energy patterns. A few individuals have apparently gained enough control over this process to be able to dematerialize and rematerialize themselves. Jesus Christ appeared to have achieved that level of mastery. Most of us, however, would settle for pulling ourselves out of a low energy period or making an illness, such as a cold, disappear.

Following is a set of activities, designed to help you develop a context for your life and work, that is broad enough to include everything in your life. These three activities are followed by a self-inventory checklist.

---

3. Personal account given to the author by a transpersonal therapist, name withheld by request of the therapist.

Activity 1 — Clarifying Your Purpose

Rationale. Your first task as a transpersonal therapist is to have a clear purpose that is broad enough to include all major areas of your life. Your purpose is defined as the overall context against which all experiences can be measured. In this way, you can always check how "on purpose" you are in what you are doing. A major criterion of success for you is the progressive realization of your purpose in life.

Step 1. Take a blank paper and write the following open-ended sentence on it: "My purpose in life is . . .." Complete that sentence, using as few words as you can that pull together all aspects of your life. An example of a purpose statement is, "My purpose in life is to experience myself as perfect, divine, and complete, and to encourage others to experience themselves in this way."

Step 2. Take your completed purpose statement and ask yourself the following questions:

Is this broad enough to include everything I do?

Will I ever complete my purpose? (purpose goes on infinitely)

Is it clear enough so you could explain it to someone else and they would understand?

Is it written in simple enough terms?

Is the statement reduced to its basic level?

If your answer to any of these questions is "no," continue playing with your statement of purpose until you feel complete with it.

Step 3. Write another purpose statement: "My purpose in being a transpersonal therapist is . . .." Complete that sentence using as few words as possible to create a context for your work. Then compare your purpose statement to the overall purpose statement you wrote in *Step 1.*

Activity 2 — Clearing Up Your Intentions

Rationale. Your intentions or wants are the motivating forces or energies that take you from your overall purpose to specific goals. The trick is to bring these energies in harmony with your purpose so your wants support your overall purpose.

Step 1. Under each of the four categories of Money, Work, Relationships, and Self-Esteem, write specific wants. (For example, under Money, you might write, "I want to be independently wealthy," or "I want enough money to pay my bills.") List as many "I wants" as you can under each category.

Step 2. Go back over each want and place a checkmark (✔) beside those that seem to support your purpose, a question mark (?) next to those you aren't sure about.

Step 3. Examine the wants that may not support your purpose and those that clearly do not support your purpose. Attempt to change them so they do support your purpose, or cross them out.

Activity 3 — Goal Setting for the Transpersonal Therapist

Rationale. Goals are ways of measuring how "on purpose" you are in an area of your life at a given time. By setting a goal, you are agreeing to give yourself a certain amount of time to find out how successful or on purpose you can be during that time frame. Many people avoid verbalizing goals because they are afraid they will be trapped by them. All goals are really made with yourself, so you can always change them if you want.

Step 1. Keeping in mind the four categories (money, work, relationships, self-esteem) used in the previous activity, write a letter to a friend and date it one year from today's date. Tell this friend all the things you accomplished in the year that just passed (which is actually the year to come). Be as specific as possible, and fantasize all the things you think might be possible for you to do during the next year. State them in the letter as if they had already been completed.

Step 2. Extract specific goal statements from the letter, and write them under each of the four categories (e.g., "I have made $50,000 this year").

Step 3. Take these specific yearly goal statements and "back them up" to six months from now. Write specific statements about where you expect to be with your yearly goal six months from today's date (e.g., "I have made $25,000 by this time").

Step 4. Reduce each goal statement to three-month and one-month goal statements. These breakdowns give you an opportunity to examine each goal again and decide whether or not you are willing to put forth the effort to reach that goal. You may wish to eliminate or change some of your goals based upon that feedback.

Self-Inventory on Attitudes of Transpersonal Counselors and Therapists

Directions: Place a checkmark in the column that best represents how you think, feel, and act relative to each statement. (Generally, your first impression is the best one.)

	Never	Sometimes	Usually	Always
a. I enjoy planning the learning of other people.				
b. I would rather learn from others than from myself.				
c. I am a good judge of what is best for me.				
d. Other people seem to ignore what I tell them.				

	Never	Sometimes	Usually	Always
e. I feel dissatisfied with myself.				
f. I see other people as being generally happy.				
g. I recognize that my thoughts create my experiences.				
h. I learn best in a formal teaching/learning situation.				
i. I don't understand why things happen to me.				
j. I see the world as generally a scary place for me and others.				
k. I have trouble seeing the unpleasant behaviors of others as a self-projection.				
l. I like myself.				
m. I worry about whether I am on the right track for me.				
n. I have trouble motivating myself to do things.				
o. I feel lonely even when I am with others.				
p. I think about all the mistakes I have made.				
q. I find that I have a lot in common with others.				
r. I have trouble spending time by myself.				

	Never	Sometimes	Usually	Always
s. I find it easy to forgive myself and others when something goes wrong.				
t. I see other people as generally able to learn from their experiences.				

Scoring Procedure:

Each item carries a weight of 1, 2, 3 or 4. In some cases, items are keyed with the "Always" column weighted at 4, and others are keyed with "Never" weighted at 4. Items scored 1, 2, 3, 4 (Never = 1; Sometimes = 2; Usually = 3; Always = 4) are c, f, g, l, q, s, and t. Items scored 4, 3, 2, 1 (Never = 4; Sometimes = 3; Usually = 2; Always = 1) are a, b, d, e, h, i, j, k, m, n, o, p, and r.

After completing the inventory, go over each item and write the corresponding number in the column where you placed a checkmark. Add all the numbers to get a personal score or identification with the attitudes of transpersonal counselors and therapists. Place this score on the continuum below and look at the suggested interpretation of your score.

```
20          40          60          80
```

Suggested Interpretation of Your Score

20-29   Little in common with transpersonal therapy concepts.
30-39   Some awareness of transpersonal therapy concepts.
40-49   Some identification with transpersonal therapists; move slowly.
50-59   Ready to proceed with learning to be a transpersonal therapist.
60-69   Go for it.
70 +   You are truly a transpersonal therapist!

A Dialogue Between the Authors

Gay: Barry, I would like to ask you a question. Do you remember a particular person or a significant event in your life that moved you in a transpersonal direction or assisted you in entering that transpersonal level in your life?

Barry: One event that I described in the chapter on developmental perspectives [chapter 3] probably did the most to open up my ideas in the transpersonal domain. That happened about twelve or thirteen years ago when I had a death in life experience. I experienced something that I couldn't explain psychologically. It transcended everything I knew at that time. I had no frame of reference to understand it. That experience, probably more than others (and there were lots of others), stands out in my mind as the one that kept gnawing at me over the last twelve or thirteen years. I found myself asking, "What did that really mean, and what was that experience telling me about myself?"

Gay: It seems to me the one thing that makes a transpersonal therapist is that he or she is willing to take experience to the limit, is willing to go all the way with a particular experience or experience in general.

Barry: I agree. I think that would characterize what I have done with that experience and many others I have had since then. Each time I've had an experience like that, I've always had a choice. I could either put it aside, and say, "I don't understand it; I don't want to look at it and deal with it," or I can go ahead and take that experience as far as I can.

Gay: . . . to be willing to experience it intensely, to the limit.

Barry: Yes.

Gay: That's one thing I think of frequently in terms of training transpersonal therapists. I come back time after time to the awareness that it is what the therapist is willing to experience that defines the quality and depth of the therapy that is going to take place. In other words, your client is only going to be able to go up to the place at which your willingness to experience has come.

Barry: I find that to be true, too. A lot of people who have come
          to me have told me that. The other day a client said she
          had experienced many events in her life — precognitions
          and things. When she had tried to talk to another
          therapist about them, the therapist told her they were
          worthless. She was admonished to not pay any attention
          to them.

Gay: The implication was that they were pathological.

Barry: Yes. The therapist put some kind of label on them that
          indicated there was something wrong with her. So when
          she brought them up again, I helped her put them in a
          context that would enable her to go through with them,
          understand them, and broaden her concept of herself, to
          include all those experiences. What she needed to do was
          not wall all that off but accept those types of experiences
          as a valid part of herself.

Gay: That's a good point. Any aspect of life that one walls off
          will eventually cause a problem, because any aspect of
          life that you disown — feelings, the past, your potential,
          telepathy, your body or spirit — is going to come back
          eventually and seek recognition.

Barry: To help people go through whatever their resistances are
          is exciting. In my own life, there are things I have
          disowned, such as rage and my own fear. When I
          understood how they are part of me, I could accept them.

Gay: When I think of those kinds of experiences in my own
          life, I remember one in particular where I became
          willing to feel fear. I kept going down into it, shaking
          with it, being with it, vibrating with it; and I kept
          choosing over and over again to feel this. I was thirty
          years old when I realized that I had never allowed myself
          to experience fear because I come from a background
          where you weren't supposed to admit you were scared.
          You were supposed to tough it out. So I had gone
          through my whole life defending against fear. When I
          got down to the bottom of the fear, I found that after a
          while I spontaneously started dancing. I happened to be
          by myself at the time, and I turned on some music and
          began to dance. Fear turned out to be something that I
          could actually dance with!

This experience taught me a lot about transpersonal therapy and a transpersonal view of life. It is those very disowned experiences that can be a tremendous source of energy once I allow them to participate in me.

Barry: Yes, I've seen it happen frequently. People who allow themselves to experience their fears suddenly transform all their fears into joy and ecstasy. What are some other experiences you've had that have moved you toward a transpersonal perspective?

Gay: I can think of a couple — one from a teacher, which really moved me. I was listening in 1971 to a talk given by Krishnamurti. In a way it was the most disquieting experience in my life, but in a way it was the most healing experience up until then, because Krishnamurti simply described the way it is in life. He described the problem carefully and came right up to the end. Everybody in the audience was saying, "Now tell us how it is going to be," "Tell us it's going to end all right." At that moment, he stopped the speech and said, "Now you must ask yourself how it is from now on. I've described the way it is right up until this moment, and now only you can be your own guru from this moment on."

It was the most electrifying thing. I practically leaped up off my seat and ran out of the auditorium. I was rattled and also healed, because he in a sense gave me permission to ask the questions myself that I wanted to know. All my life I had been looking for the answers out there somewhere.

I see that same process with my clients. My goal is to get them to experience things the way they are, not to hold out a hope that it is going to be better, or guarantee them that if they make a certain change, everything will end up all right. All I can do is say: Experience it the way it is now. The emphasis must be on developing the willingness in myself and my clients to experience life the way it is right now. I want to teach them that if they are willing to take it the way it is rather than live an illusion, they get to experience the truth that it lies just under the pain. The first thing that has to be gone through is that pain we've been holding onto, but underneath is a tremendous sense of joy and truth — a clear relationship with life.

Barry: It's deceptively easy for people to look outside themselves for the sources of their problems and also for the solutions to them. Not only are the problems inside themselves, and of their own making, but also the solutions are there. When people realize this, they are profoundly moved.

Gay: That reminds me of the other event I wanted to mention. I realize I need to see things and experience things myself now, in order to prove they are so for me. I'm no longer willing to take anybody else's word for things, unless I can personally experience them. My first occasion of seeing a transpersonal experience in action was six or seven years ago. A client I was working with was feeling scared, so I asked her to just allow herself to experience it. I had known that if I allowed myself to experience my fears fully, I would eventually come to a place of clarity that was underneath the fear, and I could get to that place only by allowing myself to experience it. I had not seen that process unfold in anybody else, so the first time it happened, I looked on in total awe as this client went down through layer after layer of fears and allowed herself just to be with it until it subsided.

Then a very amazing thing happened. Not only did she feel quiet and serene and at peace with herself, but also up bubbled a number of solutions to the problem that she was dealing with, solutions that she hadn't seen fifteen minutes before. I was profoundly moved by that because it told me once and for all that people actually do have direct access to the truth and to all the solutions they need, in themselves. It's like the statement you quoted by Richard Bach about how learning is discovering what you already know. That is such a paradox I would not have believed it until I saw it with my own eyes.

Barry: One of the things I'm interested in is how you got trained as a transpersonal psychologist. How did that happen? Was it a planned thing or did it happen accidentally? What is your perspective on that, and what do you say to people when they ask you that question?

Gay: I had a lot of training, in my formal graduate studies, in the three main forces in psychology. When I was at the University of New Hampshire, I had quite a bit of training in client-centered counseling. Then, when I was at Stanford, I had considerable training in behavioral counseling. During this time I also learned about psycho-dynamic concepts. All those approaches had value for me. In a sense, they built one on the other, and I now see that I learned many things from each of these approaches.

I eventually got to the place — I believe it was along about the time when I heard Krishnamurti talk — where I suddenly realized I had to take my own education into my own hands. So, somewhere in the early 70s, while I was still working on my Ph.D., I began seriously asking myself, "What do I really want to know?" I found that what I really wanted to know was not only psychology, but also the whole spiritual element of life. I found myself asking, "Is there a bridge between psychotherapy and spirituality?" "Is there some sort of meeting ground between those two things?" I knew that all the religious and spiritual and psychic experiences I've had must follow some kind of laws and obey certain types of principles, and I knew that all the psychological experiences I've had obey some kinds of principle, and I wanted to know where those two met. I had never heard the term *transpersonal* before that time, and I began looking around for people who also were asking these questions and whom I could discuss these things with.

At that time I met Jim Fadiman. He asked me what I was interested in, and when I told him, he said, "Oh, you're interested in transpersonal psychology." I said, "Great! Tell me about it. What is it?" He described it, and I decided I was definitely a transpersonal psychologist. He said that it was the fourth force in psychology that was being built on top of the humanistic tradition. It seemed for me the only unlimited psychology I could find. It was the only boundless one. It was the only one that seemed to reach for the sky and beyond.

After that meeting I began taking responsibility for my own education and, as a transpersonal psychologist, spent hours reading esoteric books. I spent the rest of my graduate education sitting on the floor in bookshops, reading things that I didn't have enough money to buy but wanted to read. I began reading about various Indian philosophies, Chinese philosophies, trying to find out what they were really saying about how transformation takes place. I guess the one question I kept returning to again and again was: "What is that one thing that allows transformation to take place?" Zen is talking about it. Sufism is talking about it. Freud sometimes alluded to it. I wanted to know what that one thing is that allows transformation to unfold in a person.

Barry: It sounds like a real exciting discovery process that led you to find transpersonal psychology.

Gay: Yes, it made life a lot easier to have a limitless container to hold it all in.

Barry: Yes.

Gay: How does that mesh with some of your training and background?

Barry: As you know, we come out of a similar tradition, in one sense. All of my graduate training was at the University of Minnesota, and some of your major professors were people who either taught there or were trained there also.

Gay: Yes.

Barry: The "Minnesota point of view" seems to describe how you put yourself together therapeutically and theoretically. I was exposed to all the major therapies in my graduate training. In my master's level training, like yours, I had client-centered training, and in my doctoral work I learned behavioral counseling approaches. I learned how to apply both approaches in therapy, but I didn't learn to apply psychoanalytic theory until later. I deliberately went out of my way while at the University to pick up the psychoanalytic theory of development, and then later learned how to put all that together. Like you, my process was one of constantly wanting to know more.

Even this broad framework didn't quite give me answers to the questions I would encounter with clients and the questions within myself I couldn't answer. I was seemingly led to something more complete. I felt a desire, a quest to know more. I wanted to expand the context with which I did therapy with myself and other people. Like you, I just decided to find out more and began reading articles and books in the transpersonal literature. I started to be pulled toward the transpersonal literature, and I started to understand more about aspects of my own behavior and experiences. I found that these people were asking the same questions I was asking and they were opening up areas of human endeavor that I wanted to look at. I think, more than anything else, it was the journey I was on.

Also, the one transpersonal concept that has always appealed to me, which grounds me with my own training, is that you don't want to leave any of your troops at home when working with people. It helps me to create the broadest possible context for working with people. All the other approaches would always say, "We have the answers now. You have to cast the rest aside and do what we say." I was so glad I'd found an approach to therapy that was saying to me, "Don't cast anything aside. Include it all. Learn to use it. Learn how to integrate it."

Gay: That's what I like about transpersonal psychology. It says "Yes" and gives me permission to explore and understand things that other theories just don't look at. Other approaches ignore inconsistencies or reduce them to some level of understanding that leaves out a lot of the complexities. I think it's sometimes helpful to look at behavior in that way, but it tends to be a little bit too reductionistic to handle some of the spiritual aspects of human behavior.

Barry: As I look back, a big part of becoming a transpersonal psychologist relates to my graduate training. It gave me a transpersonal perspective, because I wasn't trained in one specific approach. It encouraged me to find what works for me, to learn how to use it, and then learn how to integrate what I have learned with other things. I learned to approach therapy and the understanding of human behavior from some kind of a systematic, but expansive, point of view. I really credit my teachers at the University of Minnesota for having the wisdom to teach me that way.

Gay: I think good teachers are those who give their students total freedom and permission to go further than they themselves have gone.

Barry: I agree. The other principle they taught me indirectly was to not create a special guru for myself and to not create a mentor, whose ideas I had to overcome. They all gave me permission to do the type of things that made sense to me and not to do what they were doing exactly. It wasn't that they ever came right out and said that, but it was clear by their behavior that's what they were saying. I think that's a really valuable thing.

I remember seeing a film of Warren Bennis interviewing Carl Rogers on Rogers' seventy-fifth birthday, and Bennis asking Rogers what contributed most to his ability to develop his theory — this expansive theory of understanding human behavior. Rogers said he didn't have to overcome the teachings of a mentor, and he had permission to explore in ways that none of his teachers had taught. When I heard that, I really picked up on it and said to myself, "Yeah, that's true." I see how people can limit themselves by following a certain mentor or a certain approach.

Something is to be said for mentors, because they are good at what they do and they can achieve excellent results with a given approach. I don't want to discredit that kind of focus, but I needed something broader and more expansive — and permission to explore more complex issues in human behavior.

Gay: Barry, I've mentioned a couple of people who've been instrumental at different points in my life, either by delivering a certain message to me that I really needed to hear or by giving me a certain permission that I needed. Who were some of the significant people in your development as a transpersonal psychologist?

Barry: Really, I have to credit some of my graduate instructors
          — particularly Donald Blocher, who impressed me with
          his tremendous insight into human behavior. He's artic-
          ulate and so clear about his understanding of human
          behavior. I loved to sit and listen to him for hours just
          articulate different aspects of how to work with people.
          Also, he gave me permission to find my own niche, not
          to follow his. That was an important permission for me.

          Carl Rogers certainly influenced my thinking. I was
          profoundly interested not only in what he did but also in
          the way he did it. He certainly was a man who was
          willing to explore and to break down established bar-
          riers. He advanced our field in ways that probably we're
          just beginning to understand. He took some risks and
          did some things that nobody else in his time was willing
          to do. We wouldn't be here today calling ourselves
          transpersonal therapists had it not been for Carl Rogers.

          Maslow — although I never knew him or worked
          with him directly — had that same kind of feeling for
          psychology. Here was a man who was willing to risk
          asking questions that no one else would ask. Indirectly,
          he gave me a lot of permission to explore my hunches.

          I think of other people who briefly touched my life,
          like George Leonard, who happened to be my partner in
          an aikido class taught by Bob Nadeau. I learned so much
          in just a brief encounter with that man. He was such a
          powerful person, who knew how to channel his energy
          so effectively. Also, I remember going to an AHP con-
          vention in Berkeley and hearing a speech by Jean
          Houston. I'd never heard anyone speak as eloquently
          about psychology and human behavior. It profoundly
          moved me. I've since read some of her books and heard
          some of her other speeches, and I've always had the same
          kind of sense of here's a person who is asking the kinds
          of questions I'm asking. She's a fellow traveler in the
          transpersonal realms, and I felt a lot of kinship and
          support.

          At the same AHP Convention I remember listening
          to another speech by Leonard Orr. It was confusing for
          me to listen to. He had a very informal way of delivering

a speech — not the usual formal lecture — and while he talked, he did a lot of breathing and sighing. Part of what interested me was the audience reaction. Some people became highly incensed and walked out; some people became hysterical and started laughing at everything he said and couldn't stop laughing. I got so caught up watching the reactions of the people around me that I didn't hear much of the speech. Fortunately, I had it on tape, and I had to listen to the tape many times before I heard his message. Werner Erhard has affected me the same way. I've never taken the EST training, yet some of the things I've read that Werner has written have literally jumped off the page and hit me in a way that told me I can learn a lot from this man.

You know — I basically don't need any special teachers. My own kids are my teachers. All my clients are teachers. All my students are my teachers. All my experiences are my teachers. I'm open to learn from whoever is there teaching something.

Gay: That's one thing about transpersonal psychology. I think it opens up space for everything to be a teaching-learning situation. You can learn as much from these pine trees we are sitting among right now as you can from a particular mode of teaching or a gifted teacher.

Barry: It does seem incomplete to say these are the people who helped me get where I am. When I refer to them, they are people who stand out in my mind, and I know there were many others. I could go on naming people. I remember some of them. Others . . . I don't even know their names, but they were there. They had something — a gift to bring — not always one I wanted to receive at the time. My willingness to surrender to whatever that gift was was pretty limited. It is much less limited now.

A Transpersonal Perspective on Human Development

Barry Weinhold

The process of human development, from a transpersonal perspective, represents the broadest conceptualization of human development that I can utilize in a practical sense in my work with people. My thinking about the subject is always in a state of development, so what you are about to read represents the point to which my thinking had evolved at the time I wrote this chapter (June, 1981).

A number of attempts have been made to extend the work of traditional developmental psychologists such as Freud, Erickson, Piaget, and others to include the more spiritual, mythic, psychic aspects of human development. Maslow's hierarchy of needs was one of the approaches that postulated a higher level of development, which he termed *self-actualization.* Jung's work also added the concept of the Self, which represented wholeness and divine connections, but he looked at it exclusively as manifested during the second half of life.[1] Later, some of his followers described the Self as the original totality of the person before the ego develops.[2]

Loevinger developed a theory involving ego development, which seems to include some of the same characteristics found in Maslow's self-actualized person but which did not reach beyond that level.[3] A recent book by Wilber, *The Atman Project: A Transpersonal View of Human Development*[4], attempts to go beyond the highest level of the ego psychologists and includes a reinterpretation of their work as well as an extension of human development to include transpersonal stages.

My attempt to make some sense and order out of human development, from a transpersonal perspective, includes much of the previous work on human development done by the major psychoanalytic and ego development theorists, along with a number of humanistic and transpersonal theorists. My description of this complex, much-studied subject has to be limited here, so the following account is naturally somewhat sketchy and brief. Nevertheless, I hope to capture the essential ingredients of the process and highlight some of the key concepts.

Some unique aspects of the transpersonal perspective of human development are that:

1. Emphasis is placed on the importance of the *physical* birth process. Few development theories have, in my opinion, accounted for the importance of the birth process itself. I believe that the birth process sets the tone for all future development and, therefore, may be the most important single factor in how people develop.

---

1. See Herbert Read, Michael Fordham, and Gehard Adler, eds, *The Collected Works of C. G. Jung: Vol. 9, Archetypes and the Collective Unconscious* (New York: Pantheon Books, 1953), pp. 1-147.
2. See, for example, Michael Fordham, *New Developments in Analytical Psychology* (London: Routledge & Kagan Paul, 1957).
3. Jane Loevinger, *Ego Development* (San Francisco: Jossey-Bass, 1976).
4. Ken Wilber, *The Atman Project: A Transpersonal View of Human Development* (Wheaton, IL: Theosophical Publishing House, 1980).

2. Special attention is given to the actual bonding process, and to the long-term effects of improper bonding. Few developmental theories account for these effects in their theoretical paradigms. In the past eighteen years there have been tremendous breakthroughs in our understanding of maternal-infant bonding.

3. The *psychological* birth process is another focal point. Few theorists have looked at the psychological or second birth process, which also has tremendous implications for future development. This process could be completed as early as age two, and for most of us never is completed during our lifetime.

4. Emphasis is given to continuous development, with no break between ego development and so-called higher states of being. In this framework, transcendence is a process that occurs at each stage of development, rather than a grand and glorious event that signifies "death of the ego." The actual transcendence beyond the stage of full ego development is not seen as a quantum leap or a major break with the ego. Instead, it is seen as movement to the next higher and more integrated stage of development while incorporating everything learned from the previous stages.

5. Development is seen as sequential and presumes that any developmental task not learned at the age-appropriate time is simply carried along to the next stage, to be added to the tasks to be completed at that stage. It is always there and will remain a part of our unfinished business until it is resolved — which, for many, is later in life or never at all.

6. Age-specific stages are deemphasized. Instead, the emphasis is on completing the ego functions at each stage to better equip the person to handle the next emerging stage, with each stage leading to an eventual re-membering (uniting) who we really are and then expanding even more as a conscious unified being.

7. Special attention is directed at the problem of the tendency to inflate the ego rather than to complete the stages leading to full ego development. This refers to the tendency to look "enlightened" or God-like in place of the real thing (being enlightened and being God).

8. The newborn child is seen as highly aware and connected to the infinite, transpersonal realms of existence. This is similar to Jung's central unifying archetype, which he termed the *Self*. My contention is that if this core self or transpersonal core receives nurturing and support, it will grow and remain a vital force; if it is not supported and nurtured, the infant will become cut off from this core self. The person is then left with the difficult task of re-membering (uniting) this core self. Hubert Benoit stated the case this way:

> Man is born the son of God . . . but he is forgetful of his origin . . . Amnesic, he suffers from illusorily feeling himself abandoned by God, and he fusses about . . . in search of affirmations to support his divinity which he cannot find . . .[5]

BIRTH: THE BLUEPRINT FOR ALL FUTURE DEVELOPMENT

Until recently, most obstetrical practices were designed to rush people through the birth process as quickly as possible. The belief seemed to be that the quicker it was, the better it would be for everyone concerned. The work of the French obstetrician Frederick LeBoyer caused people to begin questioning these practices, and in the past ten to fifteen years a virtual revolution has taken place in the way we birth people.[6]

New research findings also suggest a strong need to change many traditional practices and beliefs.[7] For example, recent research has confirmed that the newborn is able to see clearly, at a rather myopic focal length of about twelve inches — the approximate distance from the breast to the face of the mother. And what has been confirmed is that the newborn is highly sensitive to all sensory stimulation, as opposed to the belief of a lack of sensory development.

---

5. Hubert Benoit, *The Supreme Doctrine* (New York: Harper, 1960).
6. Frederick LeBoyer, *Birth Without Violence* (New York: Knopf, 1975).
7. As evidence, see Joseph C. Pearce, *The Magical Child: Rediscovering Nature's Plan for our Children* (New York: E. P. Dutton, 1977).

Imagine for a few minutes what your birth must have been like. Pay attention to your reactions as you read these words describing the standard obstetrical practice still used in many hospitals: After hours of struggle made more difficult by the birthing position of your mother (feet in stirrups, lying on her back), you emerge (if not sucked or clawed) into a cold, noisy world of bright lights, semi-drugged, over-stressed, exhausted. Before you have the opportunity to take a breath on your own, you are hooked up to a respirator or held up by the heels and slapped on the back. Already out of breath from the journey, your next ordeal is to have suction devices stuck in your mouth, nose, and ears, your eyelids peeled back, letting painful light and even more painful chemicals enter your tender young eyes.

Next the umbilical cord is cut, whether you are breathing on your own or not, and then the blood from your mother's episiotomy is cleaned from your body and you are laid on cold, hard scales to be weighed like a choice roast of beef. If this isn't enough, you are then wrapped tightly in a blanket and whisked away to the nursery or incubator, either screaming in pain and terror or in a semi-conscious state from all the anesthesia administered during the birth process. If you were born in a hospital, this likely described much of what your first encounter with this world was like.

Consider what you might have learned about the world in this first encounter with it. Remember, you moved from a soft, warm, dark, quiet, totally nourishing place into a harsh sensory bombardment. You were physically abused, violated in a number of ways, and subjected to physical pain and insult, all of which could possibly be overcome if it weren't for one additional act of cruelty: You were isolated from your mother. This final barbaric act is almost impossible to overstate. No court of justice could hand out a punishment severe enough to account for this crime against helpless humanity. The final isolation from your mother robbed you of the bonding necessary to overcome the effects of your ordeal.

BONDING: A VITAL PROCESS

We now know that maternal-infant bonding, which takes place during the first twelve to twenty-four hours, is necessary for the relaxation of muscles tightened during the birth process, for full activation of the central nervous system, and for completing the reticular formation necessary for full mental-physical coordination and learning.

A newborn, if allowed to, bonds or attaches to his or her mother almost immediately after birth. The sound of her voice, the sight of her face during feeding, the feel of her skin, the smell of her body are all clear signals of safety and security in this otherwise foreign and harshly demanding world. Naturally, this attachment requires a significant amount of private father-mother-infant contact during the first several days, including skin-to-skin contact between mother and child during the first hour or so after birth. This original mother-infant bonding is the blueprint for all the infant's subsequent attachments and is the first step in the psychological birth process. Throughout your lifetime the quality of this first attachment influences the quality of all other bonds with other individuals.

Klaus and Kennell have contributed much to our understanding of the bonding or attachment process and have summarized their research findings into seven crucial components of the process of bonding.[8]

1. They found that the optimal period for bonding is the first minutes after birth on through the first hours of life. During this time they suggest maximum physical and sensory contact with the newborn, by both mother and father. They found this to be crucial for healthy later development.
2. Mothers and fathers make species-specific responses to the infant immediately after birth, and these are necessary to activate the infant's sensory attachments. For example, hearing mother's or father's voice has a critical orienting function for the infant.
3. Mother and father become attached to one child at a time. In multiple births this factor has to be taken into account so that each infant receives time alone with the parents.

---

8. Marshall Klaus and John Kennell, *Maternal-Infant Bonding* (St. Louis: C. V. Mosby Co., 1976).

4. The infant has to respond to the parents to give them a signal that they are making contact. Otherwise, they can get discouraged and withdraw, making the attachment more difficult.

5. Anyone who witnesses the birth process is likely to become strongly attached to the infant. This would suggest that the more of the immediate and extended family that can be present, the more attachment possibilities are created.

6. Mothers and fathers have difficulty attaching to an infant if that infant has some life-threatening illness or problem during this attachment period. They cannot attach freely and at the same time be worried about the threatened loss of the infant. Also, a father whose wife has life-threatening complications during the birth process would have difficulty with an attachment to the infant.

7. The parents' emotional condition during the first few hours after birth have long-term effects on the child's development. For example, a mother's anxiety about the well-being of her baby, who has a temporary illness in the first day following the birth, may result in long-lasting concerns about the health of her child, and this could adversely shape the child's development.

According to Klaus and Kennell's work, considerable care must be taken to help prepare parents to deal psychologically with the attachment process. They suggested that to not do that is to invite disaster. If something goes wrong during this early attachment process, according to their overwhelming research evidence, it will have long-term and perhaps lasting effects on the development of the child.

THE PSYCHOLOGICAL BIRTH: A CRUCIAL JOURNEY

The term *psychological birth* was used by Louise Kaplan to describe the next important developmental process.[9] This "second birth" occurs when the infant has successfully separated from the

9. Louise Kaplan, *Oneness and Separateness: From Infant to Individual* (New York: Simon and Schuster, 1978).

symbiosis with mother. The human infant at birth is not ready to take its place in the world as a fully functioning human being. The infant must be taught carefully so it can develop into a fully functioning human being. Infants who have accidentally been placed with animals at this stage have grown up with more animal than human traits. We know that the kind of teaching one gets during these early years is extremely important to subsequent development; yet, much of the teaching is random, unconscious, and narrow in focus.

Successful completion of the psychological birth process from infant to individual takes one through at least four distinct stages of development, each involving a major transformation into the next stage. The following diagram illustrates the psychological birth process starting from the physical birth. At birth, the Self is present before any ego functions develop. Gradually the ego forms, first as a separate part of the person, and finally is integrated with the Self following completion of the psychological birth.

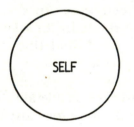

At Birth

After Bonding

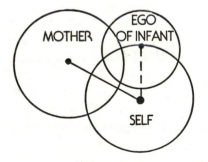

About 1 Year

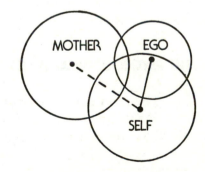

About 18 Months

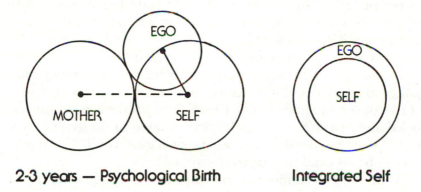

2-3 years — Psychological Birth   **Integrated Self**

Unlike the case of the inflated ego (discussed later in this chapter), the integrated Self and ego allow a wholeness of the individual to emerge. When the lower self (ego) and higher self (Self) are in harmony and not separated from each other, one always has access to the aspects of the other necessary to function effectively in most situations. This is unlike the Jungian conceptualization, in which the ego and Self are separate until later in life, when they begin to come together.

Now let's trace those early stages of development briefly so you can begin to identify with this crucial journey. As a newborn infant you moved quickly from the confused state of a stranger in a strange land to a oneness with the mothering one. This bonding or attachment was necessary for your survival. It happened both gradually and all at once, as your mother and you explored your new relationship. From your perspective, there were literally no boundaries between you and your mother. You were one. In that oneness was your security and relief from the stress and anxiety of being in a world where no one knew what you were like. At first everything seemed perfect and comfortable, but gradually you came to experience displeasure, discomfort, a return of the anxiety. By about five months you completed this initial symbiotic stage of development.

To balance the need for oneness, a strong urge to move out into the world stirred in your being. This was the beginning of your psychological birth as a separate person. By about eight months you were able to venture out a little more as you began to be able to hold constant an image of your mother even when she was not present. This object constancy would later become your major security as you ventured out further. The onset of this object constancy enabled you to begin practicing the skills you needed to develop in order to become a separate human being.

By one year your moves away from your mother became more courageous. You could walk away on your own, and you began to feel like the conqueror of your world. You jumped, ran, climbed, labeled and claimed your world. Still unable to understand that you and your mother were not separate persons, you believed your world to be an extension of your mother.

Around eighteen months you came to the wonderfully frightening realization that your mother was actually a separate person. This event more than any other heralded the crisis of your second birth. Your previously joyful mood turned into sadness and anger with the terrifying realization that you were actually alone. For the next year or two you were learning that it was possible to be a separate person without giving up your sense of wholeness. Above all, you were learning that you could still get love from your parents and hold on to a sense of self-love, too.

By about age three you developed an initial sense of yourself separate from your mother. You had become an individual, but the struggles between oneness and separateness persisted. If your image of yourself as a separate being was strong, you developed an emotional acceptance of yourself and others as whole persons. You were able to experience all your emotions, including both love and hate. You were able to reconcile your longings for perfection with the down-to-earth reality of an imperfect world. You were able to form a lasting primary relationship — a partnership of two whole multi-dimensional human beings loving and respecting each other's separateness. You had a clear sense of your boundaries as a person and knew how to function within those boundaries, as well as how to constantly expand the boundaries through increased awareness and growth. You knew how to get close to people without fearing that you would lose your identity. In short, by completing your psychological birth, you had gained the tools to function effectively in the world.

The journey just described is the ideal, the way it should have been for all of us. Unfortunately, most adults are still struggling to complete aspects of their psychological birth because of some malfunction in this process during those first two or three years.

So many things can influence this process that it is hard to document all of them. The most important factor seems to be the degree to which those around you during that time had completed their own psychological birth. They were your models and guides, so by looking at their level of functioning, we can usually tell what likely went wrong at various stages.

POSSIBLE ADULT PROBLEMS
RELATED TO THESE EARLY EXPERIENCES

Effects of the Birth Trauma

When Frederic LeBoyer was asked on a TV interview what events besides birth are important to people's development, he replied that there were no other events — only the repeated experience of one's birth trauma until it is released. What are some manifestations of the birth trauma experience?

I call one the "watch out" problem. When people are feeling uninhibitedly happy, they often shut down their good feelings in anticipation of the bad things that will follow. People actually seem to have a personal quota on how long they can feel good at any one time.

From a transpersonal perspective, another effect that seems related directly to the trauma associated with birth is the damage done to the core self, which does much to destroy the connection the child has with the universal or transpersonal. As adults, we must laboriously rebuild that connection. Stanislav Grof, in his research on therapeutic uses of LSD, found that many of his subjects relived their whole birth process, often releasing the traumatic effects of birth. He wrote that those who completed their LSD session with a reliving of the final stage of birth experienced ". . . the often dramatic alleviation or even disappearance of previous psychopathological symptoms and a decrease of emotional problems of all kinds." His patients reported having a strong recall of the odor of anesthetics used during their birth, the sounds of surgical instruments, and other clear images of their birth scene. His patients also reported ". . . feelings of enormous decompression and expansion of space. The general atmosphere is that of liberation, redemption, salvation, love and forgiveness."[10]

Breathing As a Therapy Tool

I do not work with psychedelic drugs, but I have had results similar to Grof's, in my breathing work with people. Before the term *psychotherapy* took on more medical meanings, it referred to the process of working with breathing. Through this process, some clients describe tremendous physical and psychological releases of old traumas, which resemble the descriptions of Grof's patients. Some have complete recall of the whole birth scene, including the ability to know the thoughts and feelings of those in attendance. One client reported, following a breathing session, that she saw her father at her birth, which was filled with complications for both mother and child. She said she intuitively read his thoughts to be, "If someone has to die, let it be the child and not my wife." She reported excitedly that this might explain why her father always seemed to act so guilty around her. She was relieved at this insight and began to talk to her father about what had happened. The father had actually forgotten the source of his guilt, but when the client reported what she had experienced, her father acknowledged that he did have those exact thoughts.

The breathing process I use is simple and direct. It is similar to the process Leonard Orr and others use in what they call Rebirthing.[11] Training in the process is available throughout the country through various Theta and Rebirthing centers. The names and addresses of Rebirth trainers I would recommend are included in the Appendix. I do recommend special training for those doing breath work. The study of the breath may appear simple, but it is highly complex and can require a lifetime of study to truly master.

I generally take a fairly detailed family and medical history on clients who are going to do breath work, with particular interest in

---

10. Stanislav Grof, *Realms of the Human Unconscious* (New York: E. P. Dutton, 1976), p. 152.
11. Two books explaining this process are Leonard Orr and Sandra Ray, *Rebirthing in the New Age* (Millbrae, CA: Celestial Arts, 1977), and Sandra Ray, *Loving Relationships* (Millbrae, CA: Celestial Arts, 1980).

illness and death patterns in the family. I ask them to go back at least three generations to look for common patterns. Then I form hypotheses, which the breath itself will validate or deny. I also go over expectations during the first session, to make sure clients' expectations are not too high or too low. In the first instance, they could be disappointed, and in the second instance they could become shocked and scared by what generally happens. Without creating any definite expectations of my own, I attempt to ground clients' expectations within a range of possibilities. This grounding is necessary for some and not for others.

I ask the client to lie flat on his or her back with arms at the side, being as relaxed as possible. The breathing itself consists of connected breathing in and out either through the nose or mouth without any pauses in the process. I generally ask the client to visualize a circle with the inhale being one half and the exhale the other half, with the two halves connected. The client is to pull on the inhale and let go on the exhale, without pushing out. My function during this process is to be supportive and instruct the person on minor changes to even out the breathing cycle. I also pay attention to the position of the breath and any difficulties encountered on inhale or exhale. For example, people who don't inhale fully generally don't let in the world fully and suffer from being too closed or restricted in their lives, while those who don't exhale completely tend to hold on to old hurts and get stuck in repeating many old patterns. People who can't breathe fully into the upper chest (fully expanding the upper lobes of the lungs) tend to have difficulty with expressing love or sadness; those who are "belly breathers" are more in touch with fear, anger, and sexual feelings. Many other such variations and subtleties present themselves during an observation.

Although this is a simple and direct method of working with people, the results are far from mundane. Like Grof's LSD patients, people who experience this process go through many levels of awareness and change. There are numerous physiological and biological changes along with vivid memories and psychological insights. Generally, clients experience a release from past burdens and anxieties and are often able to feel connected to their mind, body, and spirit in ways they never have through other forms of psychotherapy or spiritual practices like meditation or yoga. Many people actually experience re-membering themselves physically, psychically, and psychologically. Quite a few clients experience intense love feelings for themselves and for others as a direct result of the release they get from breath work. I generally work with people for a minimum of five to ten sessions, with instructions on how to practice the breathing between each session. This phase of the process is completed for me when clients can get approximately the same results on their own as they can get when I am there.

One of the most important times during the process comes when clients realize that they are doing this to themselves through their breathing. They often try to attribute some magic to my instructions or just my presence. When they realize that I am not doing it to them or for them, they have learned perhaps the most important lesson of life. I emphasize the importance of this learning and look for signs of their taking full responsibility for their own results.

Grounding the Awareness

Another important, but difficult, part of the process is helping clients ground the results and learn to integrate their new awareness with their everyday world. This takes time and patience, so I do a number of things to support the process. With some clients I use individual and group therapy. With others I have created a year-long seminar series to support the integration process over time. Without some form of follow-up and support, the effects either are short-lived or can lead to further confusion and, possibly, increased anxiety.

Effects of Partial Bonding

Most people are only partially bonded. This is seen most often in their safety concerns. The partially bonded person is preoccupied with checking out, "Am I safe?" while the more fully bonded person might be asking, "What is happening?" and then take appropriate action. The concern for survival, safety, and well being often forces partially bonded persons to evaluate an experience before that experience can be incorporated, or even before it is experienced. Clients might say, for example, "I don't think I'll like to do that because it sounds too hard." They tend to restrict their lives to things that are safe, and then may feel unhappy and jealous of others who seem to be able to have more fun.

Most people are busy tiptoeing through life to make it safely to death. The definition of jealousy I use with such clients is "watching others have the fun that you won't give yourself permission to experience." In working with safety issues, I get to their bottom-line fear, which is usually a fear of death. I then help them understand where they learned their fear of death, which invariably leads them to their parents and family. When they begin to see that they blindly accepted their parents' fears, they often can begin to rid themselves of these inhibiting messages.

Another common problem related to poor bonding is the inability to express anger. The underlying fear is that expression of anger will destroy or weaken the bond even more. These people often interpret unexpressed anger in others close to them as potentially damaging to their bond, and they generally attempt to placate or remove the cause of the anger. They fear that if they were to express the anger, the bond couldn't stand its expression. The result is often repressed fear, rage, and anxiety.

From a transpersonal view, anxiety in general is seen as the result of incomplete bonding. Those who over-focus on personal safety, survival, and well being are doing so to avoid the anxiety they feel from the lack of complete bonding. Comfort issues often get redefined into safety and survival issues.

Unfortunately, partially bonded children often have to deal inordinately with safety and survival issues while they are growing up, because they did not tend to get the safety information necessary to take good care of themselves. Also, studies have shown that parental neglect and abuse is twice as high in infants who were separated from their parents at birth during the optimal bonding period.

Therapy Tools

The most important intervention I can make with clients with this type of problem is to get them to experience their feelings fully and completely. Without the knowledge that can come only from experiencing their feelings fully, they will likely remain stuck. Once they experience their fears and find out that they are fears of death, they can begin to deal with the issue of their mortality. Then they can also begin to examine the process by which they acquired these fears. In all cases, the fears are learned from our parents and other significant adults in our lives while we were growing up.

Not all clients are ready to take responsibility for this area of their life. I proceed cautiously and try to keep the discussion grounded in their reality. Ultimately, it means taking responsibility for one's illnesses and death. Some people may be able to see that they caused themselves to get a cold but won't see that they could cause themselves to get cancer or to die. I call this process "unraveling your personal birth-death cycle." It generally involves some or all of the following steps:

1. Experience your fear of death and face it squarely.
2. Begin to understand where this fear came from. You were not born with it. During the birth process you may have been close to the feeling, but primarily you learned it. Sometimes I can teach people this by having them trace the major illnesses and causes of death in their family back at least three generations. The patterns are often so clear and striking that the client may begin to see the relationship between family beliefs and sickness or death.
3. Recognize that your mind controls your body. The causes of illness and death are your thoughts. The belief that death is inevitable is the largest single cause of death in all recorded history.
4. Develop a frame of mind that supports life rather than one that fears death. The use of positive affirmations to surface subconscious emotional responses can help you support life. The basic one I use is, "I am alive now; therefore, my life urges are stronger than any death urges. As long as I keep strengthening my life urges and weakening my death urges, I will continue living in increasing health and vitality." If you have any death fears, repeating this affirmation can bring these to your attention.
5. Master some so-called spiritual purification technique like meditation, martial arts, yoga, or breathing.

6. Experiment with a variety of body-mind mastery techniques such as the mastery of food and diet, physical laws (levitation through meditation), or other bodily functions such as breathing, sleeping, pulse and heart rate, temperature, and the like.
7. Visit or talk with others who are doing similar work, to get support and encouragement.

Case Examples

I would like to begin with my own story. I attended a workshop about twelve years ago in which the leader talked about how we all repress our fears of death and we hope that by avoiding any thoughts of death we can magically avoid dying. He said that he had developed a process for helping people face their fears and wanted to know how many were interested in volunteering to participate in a session to be held that evening. I volunteered, mostly because I was curious.

Along with four others who were equally curious, I received instructions that evening to imagine my own death. Each of us was asked to go through the whole process, including attending our own funeral. My only previous vivid experience with death had been that of my grandfather, who died of cancer in a hospital at the same time I was there for surgery. So I began imagining that I was dying of cancer in a hospital. Almost immediately my breathing changed, and my body began to shake and vibrate much like convulsions. At first I thought I had consciously created these bodily reactions through my breathing changes, but I soon realized that I had no control over them, and that's when the fear hit me. I thought, "My God, I must be dying." The more afraid I got, the more the shaking and vibrating continued. I began to notice that when I relaxed and stopped trying to control all this, the shaking also subsided and what I would experience was very peaceful. I remember deciding that I liked the peacefulness so much that I was just going to relax my way through the shaking and enjoy the peaceful interludes.

Gradually the peaceful times became longer and the shaking lessened until finally I sank into the most peaceful feeling I had ever experienced. I thought, "This must be what death really is."

Then I felt myself rising out of my body. I rose up to about four feet and I remember looking down and seeing my body still lying there. Finally, I rose up through the roof of the building and began to fly through dark space at an incredible rate of speed. I could see objects and bright flashes of light going past me. The colors were bright orange, blue, green, violet — all the basic colors, all vibrant and clear.

Slowly the deep blackness of space began to get lighter and lighter until my whole consciousness was filled with a brilliant light. I remember thinking that this must be the dawning of the universe. Shortly after that, everything faded and I opened my eyes to see several people crowded around me with concerned expressions. Later I found out the leader was quite worried about me and had considered trying to bring me out of my experience. He had closely observed my shaking and peaceful alternating patterns and at the final release saw my lower jaw unhinge and my closed eyes roll back into my head. I was totally unaware of any of this and was surprised at his and other people's concern.

For weeks after the experience, I didn't really know what to make of it. One day I told a friend about it and, following my description, he asked me if I had read the *Tibetan Book of the Dead*.[12] I hadn't, so he told me that what I had described was recorded in that book as the experience of people who had died and come back to relate what it was like. Since then, I have read other descriptions of people who were clinically dead and then came back. There is a strong resemblance to what I experienced.

The final piece of the puzzle came to me some nine years after that initial experience. In December, 1978, I went through a process called Rebirthing, and what I experienced during that first Rebirthing session was almost exactly what I had experienced nine years before. These and other experiences have helped me begin to piece together some hypotheses about the connections between birth and death experiences. I have come to understand the expansion and contraction of life energy forces as they flow through me and how I can experience death and rebirth as a normal everyday experience, all part of a continuous life energy

---

12. W. Y. Evans-Wentz, *Tibetan Book of the Dead* (New York: Oxford University Press, 1960).

flow. Integrating these seeming opposite energy forces has enabled me to see everything I do and say as connected.

I have worked with a number of clients who became interested in working out their birth-death cycle. One of them, Gloria, came to me after she had a breast removed following a diagnosis of cancer. While recovering from surgery and chemotherapy, she had read several books that suggested that people give themselves cancer. She was interested in exploring why she would give herself cancer. She could not understand how she could have done that.

In my work with her, which lasted over two years, I focused on helping her see the personality patterns and beliefs she had that had led to her getting cancer. At first she resisted everything I suggested, but finally she began to make contact with a long-buried part of herself that was crying out to be recognized. Having grown up in a fairly traditional upper-middle class family, only a narrow band of ideas was tolerated. She recalled having a number of thoughts and experiences, while growing up, that were labeled silly or unacceptable. Gradually, through reframing and breathing techniques, she was able to accept that part of herself she had tried so hard to suppress. Finally, she realized that the long-term suppression of her spiritual quest had led to her cancer. There were undoubtedly many quieter and more gentle reminders that went unheeded over the years, but the life-threatening roar of cancer finally got her attention.

Since then, she has worked hard to bring her spiritual side into the light of day and re-member herself. This has not been easy, and at times her spiritual courage has been put to severe tests. But each time, with support, she has been able to pick herself up and keep going. Her marriage almost crumbled several times, but she continued to broaden her context, and now she and her husband report having the best relationship they have ever had.

Effects of Incomplete Psychological Birth

If properly nurtured and supported, the psychological birth process can be completed by about age three or four. If that foundation is laid, there are usually no other insurmountable developmental hurdles. By completing this process early enough in their development, people are equipped to handle the vicissitudes of life and can learn to function at higher and higher levels of effectiveness. Unfortunately, most of our parents did not know how to facilitate the successful completion of that process, so we are still making our way through life trying to be born psychologically.

A number of problems face adults who are dealing with this issue. The most prevalent one I see is a tendency to create dependency-type relationships, or what I would call "need obligate" relationships between two persons, in which neither is a complete, separate individual and both attempt to manipulate the partner to get what they want. Generally, the way this kind of relationship operates is that I (one member) find something that you (the other member) are afraid you can't do for yourself and then I do it for you, which obligates you to me. The reason I want you obligated to me is that I can then get you to take care of me and do something in exchange that I am afraid I can't do for myself. In this way you can obligate me to stay with you as well. These relationships are filled with power plays and manipulation; they are unfulfilling but believed necessary, so they continue.

Along with dependency relationships, another persistent problem growing out of failure to complete the psychological birth is associated with constancy. *Constancy* refers to our emotional acceptance of ourselves as we are capable of feeling all our feelings and still maintaining a sense of wholeness and integrity. When constancy is weak, there is a tendency to protect our highly valued feelings from our so-called bad or unwanted feelings by splitting them off and building compartments for each. When this happens, we are unable to experience ourselves as whole and, instead, feel fragmented and disjointed in our lives. Also, we are unable to appreciate or recognize the wholeness of others. Without constancy, the apparent contradictions between oneness and separateness cannot be reconciled. Things look all good or all bad. We can feel highly elated when our image of perfection is maintained or totally crushed when it isn't. The same is true for our perception of others. We can practically worship those who momentarily help us hold onto our self-perfection image and then see the same person as an arch enemy when that person frustrates or somehow tarnishes us by his or her behavior.

Some people with weak constancy use up "perfect partners" one after another, first overvaluing them, then undervaluing them and replacing them with the next promising candidate. This search for the perfect partner is designed to cover up an inner emptiness or alienation.

Others who have weak constancy become narcissistic, filling themselves with fantasies of grandeur of how they once were or how they could become. They seek their own idealized image in a partner who adores or can be adored as what he or she wishes to be. These efforts usually fail and the narcissist turns to face his or her own emptiness and aloneness.

Resolving this issue of constancy is difficult and often takes time for adults. It means learning to accept oneself and others with imperfections. It means being able to hold onto an image of our own goodness even when we are not behaving in good ways toward ourself or others. Even more difficult at times is to be able to maintain a positive self image when someone close to us is disapproving of our behavior. It means learning to tolerate our ambivalence toward ourselves and others and seeing everyone with both strengths and weaknesses.

Therapy Tools

Because of the tendency to see themselves or others as either over-adequate or under-adequate, clients might be asked to make a list of anything at first; then, with some help they can begin to develop an awareness of "adequate" from their perspective without any distortions. This is useful in a group therapy setting, with others giving feedback and support to the process.

Another tool I use is to help clients begin to focus on similarities, instead of differences, between themselves and others. Because people with constancy problems are alienated from themselves, they generally manage to alienate themselves from others. One of the most common means of doing that is by looking for ways in which they are different from others. I have had profound results from teaching clients to practice this "focusing on similarities" exercise. They can do it anywhere: while watching TV, waiting in line at the bank or supermarket, attending a sports event, or being with people they meet for the first time. If one is successful at teaching this skill, a person begins to see all his or her experiences as related and connected rather than fragmented and unrelated.

It is also important to help clients learn to be vulnerable with you in your sessions, and this often generalizes to other relationships. If they can come to recognize that you accept the good and bad in them and still like and respect them, they often begin to heal splits in their self image.

The Fusion Issue

Fusion with the parental energy represents another devastating effect of failing to complete the psychological birth process. From the initial bonding, there is a fusion with mother's energy. Generally, as the drive toward separateness increases and functional autonomy occurs, this fusion collapses. If it doesn't, the child remains dependent on mother's cues to help him or her decide things and, later, substitute mothers also serve to maintain this fusion. As Ken Wilber put it, "The person goes through life never daring to entertain an original idea and never daring to strike out on his own. Fusion reigns: development stops, differentiation stops, transcendence stops."[13]

When dealing with fusion issues, I use a process similar to the one I use with recycled development issues as described in chapter 8 (on relationship therapy). It is difficult to get someone who is dependent to take action on his or her behalf, but that is what I aim for, even in small ways, from the beginning. A great deal of patience and support are necessary to help clients take risks. Helping them make contact with unspoken feelings and teaching them how to express these feelings are important. This learning is a big first step in becoming separate from the parental energy.

THE SPECIAL CASE OF THE INFLATED EGO

One of the common traps that people seeking transcendence often fall into is their learning how to appear enlightened instead

---

13. Wilber, *Atman Project*, p. 140.

of solving the problems that block true enlightenment. The "inflated ego" appears to be a case of splitting related to poor object constancy.[14] As a transpersonal therapist, I seem to see more people with this problem than any other. And other transpersonal therapists likely see a number of clients who have split off from their "dark side" and are trying to elevate their higher Self and identify solely with their God-like qualities. Ken Wilber's entire thesis surrounds this issue. He explained that people make a mistake in not accepting that their core Self *is already God* and, instead, trying to inflate the ego to look like God. This he termed humanity's Atman Project.[15]

People who have fallen into this trap are recognizable in a variety of ways. In general, when individuals are attempting to operate out of some superior attitude, inflation of the ego is probably behind it. Those who are truly enlightened have no need to tell how enlightened they are or to try to gain power over others. Any power orientation that attempts to define reality for others likely has some omnipotence behind it. An attempt to equate one's own private truth with universal truth (as in writing a book like this one) is likely rooted in ego inflation. Those who come from a context of discovery instead of a context of justification generally avoid most inflationary tendencies. The more obvious examples of ego inflation are overly critical persons who always find others less able or people who use temper tantrums to get their way.

The myth of Icarus from Greek mythology is a prime example of inflation. Daedalus and his son, Icarus, were in prison in Crete, and Daedalus made them each a pair of wings so they could escape. Daedalus warned Icarus not to fly too high or the sun would melt the wax on his wings. Icarus became so exhilarated over his ability to fly that he forgot his father's warning and flew too high. The wax melted, and Icarus went crashing into the sea. This is the common problem with the inflated ego: a misjudgment of situations.

There is a *negative* ego inflation also, as exemplified by the person who identifies with the justified victim who feels trapped

---

14. Read E. F. Edinger, *Ego and Archetype* (Baltimore, MD: Penguin, 1972), for a full discussion.
15. Ken Wilber, *The Atman Project*.

and is rendered helpless by the actions of another. Ego inflated persons may also inflate their feelings of distrust or guilt. Sometimes a person alternates between the two extremes.

One such client came to me with a rather bizarre set of physical symptoms, as well as an obvious attitude of superiority in her relationships. The initial physical symptoms were an intense burning in the chest, partial loss of hearing, dizziness, constipation, and skin rashes. In working with her, I discovered that she was verbally and sexually abused as a child. She believed that she was treated so badly because she was a bad person. Therefore, she identified with the aggressor (her mother) to avoid feeling the guilt. Her feelings emerged in the physical symptoms. If she suffered long enough physically, she could absolve herself of the guilt. Of course, that only worked temporarily until the guilt built up again. She actually believed she was so bad that she drove her father away; because of that, she could not have effective male-female relationships. She began to identify with her mother to the extent that when she looked in the mirror in the morning, she saw her mother's face, not her own.

One of the ways I began to help her break down her identification with her mother was by asking her to make a list of the positive and negative ways in which she was the *same* as her mother and the positive and negative ways in which she was *not* like her mother. At first, all her negative traits and most of her positive traits were like those of her mother. Gradually, we worked to fill out the matrix so she could begin to look in the mirror and see herself instead of her mother. She began to take purposeful action on her own behalf, setting limits in relationships. Almost all her physical symptoms disappeared. Occasionally they still reappear, but they don't last long because she now has learned effective ways to deal with her feelings.

AN EXPERIENCE OF LOVE

No spiritual journey, however high or enlightened, can teach people how to love. Love of self and others comes from an emotional level, while loving God comes from a spiritual level. I usually start working with people on an emotional level to help them experience love coming from within themselves. This can form the basis for experiencing a deeper, more transpersonal love. A transpersonal kind of love can emerge only from acceptance of self and others, true forgiveness of self and others, and with compassion. These are hard things to teach anyone, but I often use imagery, metaphors, breathing exercises, or affirmations to help nurture that experience.

The following is a guided imagery exercise that I use frequently with clients to help them lift the barriers to loving themselves. I often use this in conjunction with breathing exercises to help people relax. Background music is sometimes added to create a receptive mood. My favorite is Pachlebel's "Canon in D."

Ask the client to lie on his or her back and get comfortable. Give the following instructions:

"Every relationship begins with your relationship with yourself, and initimacy with yourself sets the foundation for all relationships. In our preoccupation with others, we often forget that the basis of a very loving relationship is our loving relationship with ourself.

"It seems to be a paradox of human existence that the degree to which we are enabled to love another human being corresponds directly with our ability to love and affirm ourself. Only when we are loving ourself can we truly love and risk and be "self-less" in a relationship with another person.

"Our society/culture/family/experiences all tell us that to love ourselves is to be selfish. But selfishness is the very opposite of self-love or selfness.

"The central goal of this activity is to help you learn to reach and love the self where your love and power are integrated naturally. This starts by asking you to adopt a kindly, accepting, positive attitude toward your core self. Most people feel they really do love themselves, but deep down the exact opposite may be true. We may be afraid to confront/explore, in an understanding/loving manner, those areas of ourselves that we fear. Carl Jung wrote that the 'least of my brethren is me.'

"Imagine for a moment (with your eyes closed) that you are another person, whom you truly love. In your mind's eye, get up and sit down in front of yourself facing yourself. Ask yourself these questions and then wait for the honest answer: Do I really try to recognize, accept, and respect this person's feelings — honestly? Am I aware of this person's gifts, talents, exciting potential? Or do I only remember/recognize the mistakes, the imperfections? Am I aware of the reality of this person's limitations and willing to learn from the mistakes and failures rather than be crushed by them?

"Am I listening to this person — the feelings, intuitions, insights? Do I listen to this person's body, its needs, and what promotes its wellness? Do I play with this body, and am I aware of ways I can love it? Do I recognize this person as a gift, a cause for celebration, exactly as this person is? With the holes, the brokenness, the incompleteness, too? Do I forgive this person, think of this person as gently and lovingly as the others I love?

"By asking you to focus on yourself in this way, I am not talking about narcissism or preoccupation with self. This is merely a description of a balance, where you show the same concern for yourself that you show to a neighbor or to those you love most.

"If you do this, you know what it means, don't you? It means you have to continue to look **you** in the eye, and it takes courage to see that you are not whole yet. You have to embrace the truth about you. You're going to see the evil, the impatience, the greed, the jealousy, the pessimism, the unkindness, the fear. And, then, when you get over the horror, you'll have power — the greatest power, really. The truth will set you free because it brings love. Forgiveness gets you high, because if you see you as you are, and love it all, you can accept and love and affirm that in the other. Denying faults or limitations merely strengthens their hold on you and makes you feel more powerless. Recognizing your limitations takes the poison away and destroys their hold on you.

"The feeling of being in love with yourself doesn't imply that you have risen above all your faults and emotional problems. It merely implies that you refuse to be paralyzed by them. When you realize this, you can love yourself and someone else without strings, games, fear, or exploitation. Then you can truly rejoice in and celebrate your own uniqueness and goodness. Go in peace."

How Transformation Works:
The Physics of Willingness

Gay Hendricks

To understand the process of transformation as it applies to human psychology, we can draw on some of the basic processes of the universe identified by physics. Physics is the envy of all the sciences because it deals with only a handful of major variables and because its theories often fit the facts quite snugly. This is in contrast to fields like biology and psychology, which both have a seeming infinity of variables and, correspondingly, more difficulty in fitting the findings with the predictions. Physics has refined its field of inquiry down to a few all-encompassing notions like matter, energy, and space. We can learn from physics by applying concepts of matter, energy, and space to our field, psychology, and its use in transforming human personality.

Let us begin by assuming, as physics does, that the function of everything in the universe is expansion and contraction. There is only one thing in the universe, everything is made of it, and what it is doing all the time is expanding and contracting. Right now, in our part of the universe, or perhaps everywhere at this time in the universe, the major process that is happening is expansion, although there are sub-themes of contraction within this larger context of expansion. This is roughly what Einstein said, and it has been supported by many findings since his original conception of the theory of relativity. In the most practical terms, right now in evolution, the counselor, whose role it is to teach effective processes of living, must know a lot about expansion and something about contraction.

WHERE PROBLEMS COME FROM

When expansion and contraction occur freely, we get to experience life as a process, a dance. When expansion and contraction are resisted, however, life becomes static, and the dance grinds to a halt. The reason for this is that right now in evolution, human beings appear to have an overlay on the basic process of expansion and contraction. This overlay provides resistance, a drag on expansion and contraction, which, while it does not stop the process, decreases enjoyment and oneness with the process so that we feel estranged from ourselves, others, and the universe. The overlay is experienced in many ways — as thoughts like, "Should I be having this experience?" or, "Am I doing it right?"; as body phenomena like tension and rigidity; as feelings like confusion and fear.

What do expansion and contraction feel like? Expansion feels like freedom, breathing easily, outflowing love, a sense of self-direction, space, permeability. Contraction feels like pain, density, a sense of being the effect rather than the cause of things, drivenness, constriction. In the terms that physics gives us (matter, energy, space), we can regard contraction as matter and expansion as space. Energy is the transition between mass and space, or the rapid alternation of the two, and is experienced as excitement, confusion, vibration, movement, dissolution. Whether or not you enjoy energy, matter, or space depends on how you feel about them.

In practical terms, *mass* can be regarded as those things we cling to, such as structures, beliefs, opinions, patterns from the past, old feelings. *Energy* is experienced when we let go of those dense elements of ourselves and begin to move toward space, or when we leave space and move toward contraction. We experience *space* when we have expanded enough to feel that we are the container, or context, for mass and energy.

While the mind, trained to be judgmental, may try to regard expansion as good and contraction as bad, note that we are all in the process of expansion and contraction all the time. If you doubt this fact, pay attention to your breathing for a few moments. Our task as therapists, then, is not to teach people that they should be expanded all the time but, rather, to assist them in becoming masters rather than slaves of the entire expansion-contraction process.

When people let go of their resistance and begin to feel comfortable with the process of expanding and contracting as a whole, they are on their way to mastering the most fundamental process of life.

Because of Einstein's theory, and because one can readily check out the process in one's own life, we can say with confidence that the overall context for life right now in evolution is expansion. Things seem to be headed in the general direction of increased freedom and space, though not without sub-themes of contraction within the larger process. To teach our clients how to feel comfortable with the overall process of expansion and contraction, then, is to help them get in step with the way things are. The attitude that allows one to feel good about the basic process of expansion and contraction, along with the transition/energy state, duplicates in the individual the larger cosmic process. When the full process is allowed to unfold with confidence in the larger process of expansion, life becomes much smoother. Difficulties arise when we put brakes on during one part or another of the process. When we slam on the brakes during the experience of energy, for example, it roughens up our experience of it, so that what could be felt as excitement is felt instead as fear. The process itself continues to take place, of course, regardless of our experience of it but enjoyment and benefit from the process suffer.

To use another example, you may feel angry at someone. If you allow yourself to expand with the experience of the anger, it may be over in a moment. If you put the brakes on, because of an overlay that says, "I shouldn't feel angry," or a tension in your shoulders, you perpetuate the anger and hold it in place. By resisting it, the contraction intensifies until it becomes painful.

Similarly, when expansion is resisted, the experience of it gets rougher. I know of a woman who developed cancer. After ordinary medical treatment failed, she decided to take responsibility for it and heal it herself. As she began to inquire into the illness, she saw that she had been denying her own growth and need for stimulation. She had sacrificed her own education so she could support her husband, and she had put aside other growth experiences in favor of her church and children. It became clear to her that the cancer, indeed a form of growth, was an unhealthy expression of something that actually could have been expressed positively had she been willing to open up to it. After she explored these ideas, she decided to make some changes in her life that would allow healthier kinds of growth. The cancer disappeared. Her physician said it was a "spontaneous remission." Her minister called it a miracle. She, who had taken responsibility for it, had a better explanation.

WILLINGNESS ————————————————————

When we are unwilling to experience, we are resisting what is. To resist experience is to hold the universe at arm's length. Being willing to experience opens us up so we can embrace the universe.

Willingness also has the effect of doing away with the limitations of time and space. If you are unwilling to experience fear, for example, you must march linearly through time, creating one opportunity after another to feel scared until you can learn not to resist it. When you become willing to experience it, you do away with the need to create future experiences of it, because you are willing to feel it now. Once you are willing to deal with something now, time does not matter. Space ceases to be an issue as well. If you are willing to deal with the problems in a relationship right here and now, it does not matter that the person is 2000 miles away.

Similarly, if you are willing to solve a given problem, the solution has space to emerge in an appropriate time. To use a recent example from my own life, I arose one morning to write this chapter. Then I realized I did not want to. When I examined my reasons and my feelings, I realized I was tired, I wanted to think about some other projects, and the ideas themselves had not become clearly formulated in my mind. At first I resisted and started to force myself to sit down and write. Then I saw what I was doing and let myself surrender to my own experience. I rested for a few minutes and let my mind turn to other projects. Quickly, though, in a sudden burst of thoughts, what I wanted to say in this chapter emerged in my mind in a totally different form, one with which I felt much more satisfied. This flow of creativity did not happen until after I had given myself permission not to think of the subject at all.

THE DOORWAY TO TRUTH AND LOVE

Unwillingness to experience takes us away from the here and now. Willingness brings us into the present, where we have access to a true creativity that is not burdened with the past.

At the moment we become willing to experience *what is*, we are connected to truth and, ultimately, to love. If I am feeling sad, and unwilling to experience it fully because of the strictures of my past conditioning (e.g., "Big boys don't cry"), I am distanced from the truth of my own experience. There is a veil of someone else's reality between me and mine. At the moment I become willing to experience things as they are, I move to the doorway of love through letting myself feel the truth.

Not until I can see things the way they are do I have the opportunity for a clear experience of love. Love depends on space, and space can come about only through willingness. Until I am willing to experience others as they are, I cannot grant them the space in which love can emerge. As Einstein said, "Space is love." We may regard the converse, "Love is space," as true, also. The type of love that does not simultaneously give space can hardly be called love. It is certainly of little value in therapy.

We cannot try to love our clients. If effort is present in the situation, there is no space, no love. If we find ourselves making efforts to love, we need to fall back and work on loving ourselves more so that we can get beyond *doing* and simply let ourselves *be* love.

To experience love, for ourselves and others, is the most powerful therapeutic environment we can create.

5

The Therapeutic Value of Being

Gay Hendricks

Philosophers from Socrates to Sartre have tried to define *being* and to understand its seeming all-important contribution to the quality of life. Their attempts have perhaps been successful in philosophers' terms but have not helped us understand the role of *being* in therapy. Because I believe that effective therapy depends on the quality of being in the therapist, I would like to share, in the most practical terms possible, what I have learned about being over many years of dealing with the issue in the counseling relationship.

WHAT IS BEING? _____

I like to think of being as the amount of space the counselor is willing to occupy. If we think of being as space, and of what we are doing as those things that fill the space, we can see that it is *doing* (the things that fill space) that traditionally gets more of our attention than space itself. Space seems invisible, hard to measure, impossible to define. Yet we now know, thanks to people like Einstein, a few facts about what space is and what rules it seems to follow.

In therapy terms, we all must acknowledge that who the therapist *is* makes the difference — not what he or she does. I have seen Fritz Perls do a Gestalt empty-chair episode with a client, and I have seen Perls' imitators do the same type of exercise. The difference was profound, both in the quality of the moment-by-moment experience and in the results they got. I have also seen totally unknown and unsung therapists who, by the quality of their presence and attention, assisted their clients in "moving mountains." In my own work, I have done the same type of activity with various clients. The quality of my being was so different in each case that both the way I felt about the session and the results I got were different.

I have also experienced many times a phenomenon that never fails to move me. I will be working with someone, and it will be slow going. I may be bored or tired or preoccupied with some issue that has nothing to do with what I am doing in the moment. Suddenly I will notice the low quality of being that I am presenting, and I bring my attention fully to the present. I drop my bored or tired or preoccupied point-of-view and focus on the moment. Then there is a shift in what is going on in the interaction with my client as well. The air seems fresh again. The client becomes more intense. Movement occurs.

What, specifically, is being? What determines the amount of space the therapist occupies? I think there is one major determinant: the therapist's *willingness to experience.* How willing the therapist is to experience feelings, the body, growth, change and, ultimately, love determines how far the client can get with the same issues while in the therapy relationship.

In the therapy relationship, therapists are constantly challenged to expand their willingness to experience. In the realm of feelings, a client may present a problem in dealing with anger. What happens if the therapist is also stuck on anger? If the therapist has only limited strategies for dealing with anger, the client may not learn (with this therapist at least) how to experience anger fully, express it appropriately, and come to love it. So it is the therapist's willingness to experience feelings, to allow them space to *be*, that is a major contributor to the quality of *being* in the relationship.

In the realm of the mind, a similar principle holds true. Here, the major willingness that is required is for the therapist to hold diverse points of view and to be willing to let go of points of view and be free of them. The therapist enhances the quality of being by allowing space for various points of view and by being willing to jump off into space with no point of view to hold on to. By doing these things in the therapeutic relationship, the therapist sets an example that is of utmost importance to the client. The client may experience directly that it is permissible and possible to be large enough to hold different points of view, to make one's home in space.

In the realm of the body, these issues take on an added dimension, one that has only recently been explored in therapy. The quality of being, in the therapy relationship, appears to depend on how much space therapists are willing to occupy in their bodies. To assess this level of willingness, therapists must ask themselves questions like the following:

How aware am I of my body?
How much love do I feel toward my body?
Are there parts I do not love? What are they? How did I come to disown them?
What limiting patterns and postures do I hold in my body?
Is my body tuned up enough to be my friend?
How can I best use my body as a therapeutic instrument?

One of my students was working with a person who was struggling to open up to some grief she had been holding for a long time. As I watched the videotape, I noticed that my student had his chin pulled down nearly to his chest and was not breathing deeply. He was a perfect mirror of the client's posture, although he was unaware of it. I asked him how much of his own sadness was hooked by the client's, and he acknowledged that the client's sadness did indeed bring up some previously unexplored sadness of his own.

In the next session, I asked my student to be aware of his breathing and his posture so that he could use his own body to show the client that she could open up to her grief. Although the student had been telling her verbally that it was okay to experience her sadness, he had been broadcasting with his body that she should stay closed to it. The difference in the next session was striking. The client began exploring the sadness, and part way through the session had a major catharsis. Although we cannot say for sure what made the difference, I can report that my student's chin was up and he was breathing deeply throughout the session.

Another aspect of being is how much room there is for growth in the therapy relationship. Here, Maslow's hierarchy of needs[1] comes into play. We must keep in mind that it is normal to work one's way up from survival through successful ego development, then on to self-actualization and transcendence. But we must not let our view be limited by a linear model of growth. For maximum movement to take place in therapy, it is essential to make space for total transformation to occur at all times. In this way we can charge the air with the greatest possible therapeutic potential. Some clients have limited goals for therapy, as do some therapists. Regardless of the client's goals, it is to everyone's advantage for the therapist to have extraordinarily high goals. Then clients have the opportunity to be in the presence, at least once in their lives, of someone who sets no limit on how much they can be.

Perhaps above all other considerations is the therapist's willingness to experience and express love. The quality of *being* in the therapy relationship could well depend at heart on the amount of love that can be felt and shared by therapists and clients. Love is certainly the most powerful tool for transformation that I have ever experienced. I have seen shattered people come to unity through love. I have experienced long-disowned parts of myself come into harmony with me again by becoming willing to love them.

---

1. This hierarchy is illustrated on page 6, and discussed in Abraham H. Maslow, *The Farther Reaches of Human Nature* (New York: Viking Press, 1971).

I would vote for willingness to give and receive love as the ultimate lesson we need to learn, both in therapy and life itself.

In regard to being, love may be the ultimate creator of space, since it always contains within it what is not loved. In thirteen years of doing therapy and training therapists, I have never seen anyone go wrong by loving more.

IN CONCLUSION

Counselors cannot be expected to be flawless in regard to their willingness to experience feelings, body, mind, unconditional love. But they must be at least willing to look at their barriers to experiencing complete willingness in all areas of life. If counselors have complete willingness as a goal, and are willing to explore anything that is in the way, the therapy relationship is charged with the aliveness of an ultimate potential for growth.

6

Transpersonal Uses of Human Energy Patterns

Barry Weinhold

As a transpersonal therapist, one of my tasks has been to broaden and deepen my understanding of human behavior and at the same time look for, in all theoretical systems, common elements that provide simple and direct ways to understand behavior. In my work with people, I seek the most direct ways that enable me to understand and predict their behavior at all levels. My search for these common elements has led me repeatedly to the study of human energy patterns. During this study, I have found several basic operating principles that have proven useful:

1. Human energy is always moving. It is either expanding or contracting.

2. Any resistance to either the expansion or the contraction of energy causes problems. The flow of energy has a natural rhythm, and when we resist the flow, we use up considerable energy and create problems for ourselves.

3. Thoughts are a basic form of energy and seem to influence the expansion or contraction of energy fields. Paranoid thoughts tend to produce contraction, while harmonious thoughts tend to produce expansion of energy fields.

4. Feelings are another basic form of energy and, similar to thoughts, influence the expansion and contraction of energy. For instance, fear causes contraction and love causes expansion.

5. Most people are not tuned in to their own or other people's energy patterns. They have to be taught and, once taught, can master their own energy patterns.

6. The source of all our energy is our transpersonal core. Contact with this core without undue "noise" or interference of energy pulsations from the core allows for free and complete energy flow and energy exchange.

Six different patterns that I work with when doing therapy are described in the following pages. I may never use all six of these with a single client, although I frequently do have to touch on all six and then focus on one or two patterns. The six patterns are: (1) gaining awareness of human energy patterns, (2) releasing blocked energy patterns, (3) creating new energy patterns, (4) protecting vital energy patterns, (5) sharing creative energy patterns, and (6) balancing all life energy patterns.

GAINING AWARENESS OF HUMAN ENERGY PATTERNS

Most clients, I find, have little awareness of their own energy patterns, or no awareness at all. I generally do some telling (explaining the basic operating principles) and a lot of showing, helping them to experience their own energy. Usually it is necessary to create a context for this awareness or I can end up wasting my own energy. Brugh Joy put it this way: "I dare to say that the human mind can and does generate force fields that can transmute matter. I further dare to say that an awareness without spiritual foundation is like a stool with only two legs"[1]

There are at least four main areas of awareness: (1) energy fields surrounding the body, (2) energy that flows through the body, (3) energy imbedding in the surface muscles of the body, and (4) energy in the deep muscle structure of the body. To illustrate these, I show my clients a number of high quality kurlian photographs of human energy fields.[2] In addition, I use some simple energy awareness techniques, such as the following.

Hand Excitation

I ask clients (singly or in a group) to stand in a relaxed position and shake their hands vigorously for about thirty seconds to a minute, then to place their hands about six inches apart, with palms facing each other, and notice the energy flow between them. After doing this several times, they might do it with you or another person. They are usually fascinated and eager to learn more.

Changing Energy Flow

Another way to dramatically demonstrate the principle of thought energy and how thoughts can change energy patterns involves an aikido technique. I generally demonstrate the use of thought to change the direction of energy flow.

I have clients stand and imagine their energy moving downward through the bottom of their feet, rooting them to the floor. Then I ask them to imagine actual roots growing out of the bottom of their feet and extending deep into the ground. After that, I try to pick them up or ask another person to try it. I then ask them to

---

1. W. B. Joy, *Joy's Way: A Map for the Transformational Journey* (Los Angeles: J. P. Tarcher, 1979), p. 129.
2. Thelma Moss, *The Probability of the Impossible* (Los Angeles: J. P. Tarcher, 1974).

reverse their energy and imagine it flowing out of the top of their head, making them light and airy. I have them envision themselves actually lifting off the ground as I try or a partner tries to pick them up. The contrast is always noticeable, and sometimes very striking. I have clients do the same process with me or a partner so they are able to be on both ends of the experience.

The Universe Always Says "Yes"

This is another of my favorite activities to help clients realize that thoughts are energy and that these thoughts manifest into experience. The basic premise is that whatever you are thinking at the moment is always supported by the universe, which is saying "yes" to what you are thinking. The universe doesn't care about the quality of your thoughts; it is basically neutral. If you are critical of yourself, the universe will support your self-criticism the same as when you are loving toward yourself.

Step 1. Have clients pair off with a partner or with you. One is the universe and is to answer "yes" to everything the other person says. As a way of directing the process, I ask participants to share at least three common negative thoughts they have about themselves. After each one, the universe is to reply, "Yes, that's true," or "Yes, Sam, you are selfish," for example. If you are doing this process with two clients, have them switch roles so both will get to experience their self-defining words.

Step 2. Next have clients relate three positive thoughts they have about themselves, using the same procedure as in step 1.

Step 3. Ask them to tell the universe (the partner) something they want to change in their lives. The universe is to reply to that by saying, "Yes, you do want to change _____." Again have the two switch roles.

Step 4. This step is designed to help people see that wanting something is a thought barrier to having it. This time have clients restate each statement in step 3 as if it had already taken place. This would mean changing, for example, "I want to have more friends" to "I have all the friends I want." Again the universe partner is to reply and support this thought energy.

Step 5. Sometimes I go even further and have clients write out their statements of step 4 and then jot down any resistant thoughts that surface. These resistant thoughts constitute "noise" that prevents clear communication of the thoughts with the universe. For example, a resistant thought that might surface from the statement in step 4 is, "What if people don't want to be my friend?" Then I ask them to think of another thought that would dislodge that resistance. In this example, a thought that could dislodge the resistant one is "The people I choose as friends also choose me." Don't forget to have the universe partner affirm that thought as well.

A variation of the above activity is to simply ask clients to state what they want. Ask them to repeat the open-ended sentence, "What I want is . . . ." Use the same affirming procedure as above.

RELEASING BLOCKED ENERGY PATTERNS

Frequently, chronic energy blocks show up in the body. If energy has been blocked in a muscle grouping, for example, there will be a shortening of that muscle or certainly a tightness or tension in that part of the body. Some of the "early warning signals" may be a stiff neck, tight shoulders, head ache, leg ache, or stomach ache. If people ignore these signals, they get stronger, perhaps resulting in an illness of some kind. I believe through experience that all illness or disease in the body can be traced to a belief or thought pattern that interrupted the energy flow in the body.

For example, arthritis can be traced to holding on to long-term resentment or bitterness over not being loved the way we wanted to be. Cancer comes from deep grief and hurt and long-standing resentment. In both cases, the problem is in the *holding on*, so I see my major task in helping with these diseases to help clients learn how to release whatever they are holding on to.

I use a variety of techniques to promote this release. I often use stress postures from bioenergetics, yoga, breathing (neo-Reichian or Rebirthing), imagery, writing processes, movement and dance, meditation, and even art or music as a way of helping clients recognize and release blocked energy.

To initially diagnose blocked energy patterns, one successful means I have found is to have clients draw a front view, full body picture of themselves on a large piece of newsprint. Then I take a Polaroid picture of them. In comparing the two pictures, the photograph usually reflects what they have drawn. For example, if a client were to draw himself or herself with one shoulder lower than the other, the same misalignment would probably show up on the photograph. I go over the photos and the drawings with clients and have them write hypotheses on the drawings. In the case of the lowered shoulder, a client might write, for example, "Right shoulder higher to protect that side of my body." I like this method because it gives the client feedback in a usable form, and it gives me useful information as well.

Another good tool is to use videotape to do such diagnoses. This allows reflection of the way clients walk, sit, stand, and move.

The most useful diagnosis tool is simply learning to read bodies. With a trained eye, one will get everything needed, through simple observation. Milton Erickson, the great hypnotherapist, was an astute observer of nonverbal behavior, as was Fritz Perls. Erickson reportedly once paid a pantomime expert to teach him all the ways he knew to say "no" nonverbally.

Briefly, these are among the things I look for in bodies in order to form hypotheses:

1. How individuals walk: Which foot do they start on? Starting on the left foot generally means a person is more passive when stepping out into the world, while starting with the right foot indicates more aggressive moves. I then look for problems associated with being too tentative (left foot) or too aggressive (right foot).

2. Body proportions: A heavy upper body and thin lower body usually indicates a lack of grounding or more armor or protection of upper body functions. Feelings may be suppressed. A heavy lower body and thin upper body can mean a number of things as well. Generally it means too much grounding and an inability to flow with things.

3. Misalignment left to right side or front to back: A raised shoulder also can be accompanied by a raised hip, with the

90

whole body compensating for one part being out of alignment. A raised left shoulder tends to be used to protect feelings, particularly love feelings. A pelvis tilted back can indicate repressed sexual feelings or sexual fears.

4. The face: Puffiness under one eye might indicate problems with thinking or feeling. The left eye is an indicator of emotional problems and the right eye, thinking problems. The eye in which tears form first often provides an interesting clue. If tears form in the left eye, the person is feeling sad; if they form first in the right eye, the person is feeling angry or scared. In almost every case where I have verified the feeling, this has held true.

5. Breathing: Watching how people breathe can tell a lot. For example, people who seem to hold on to their exhaling breath generally have more trouble than usual in letting go or flowing with things; they tend to be more uptight and anxious, too. People who have a rather weak inhaling breath generally don't let in much of the world and often have impoverished or limited experiences; they tend to exhibit more depressive symptoms.

CREATING NEW ENERGY PATTERNS

Many people whom I see don't appear to know how to create energy for themselves when they need it. Frequently, they have learned to compensate for this by "stealing energy" from others. This works for them at times, but it means that they have to create dependency relationships in order to have someone available when they need an energy boost. The dependency relationship itself requires considerable energy to maintain, so they may end up using more energy than they can steal at times.

People can be taught, through a number of methods, how to generate new energy on their own. These methods include a variety of meditative techniques, various yoga forms, the martial arts (particularly the forms that focus on inner awareness), exercise programs such as jogging or swimming, some nutritional and diet programs (particularly if a person is overweight), breathing exercises, writing processes, guided imagery, and visualization techniques.

Often I use meditation and breathing exercises myself to generate new energy when I am feeling low in energy. I can use these while being with clients as well. One such structured experience I call the cleansing breath.

The Cleansing Breath

Step. 1. Have clients sit or lie on their back with eyes closed, breathing in and out through the nose. Ask them to pull in the inhaling breath and let go of the exhaling breath, connecting both inhale and exhale.

Step 2. After they have developed a breathing rhythm, ask them to concentrate on breathing in *light* on inhale and breathing out *toxins* on exhale. Have them do this for five or six breaths.

Step 3. Now ask them to breathe in *strength* and breathe out *tension* for another five or six breaths.

Step 4. Ask them to breathe in *love* and breathe out *fear* for another five or six breaths.

Step 5. Finally, ask them to breathe in *light, strength,* and *love* together and breathe out *toxins, tension,* and *fear.* Have them take five or six long, deep breaths, filling their body with light, strength, and love and emptying their body of all toxins, tension, and fear.

This short breathing exercise (five to ten minutes) is useful if clients begin to show signs of low energy during sessions. After teaching it to them, I recommend that they use it when they feel they need more energy during their daily routine.

Meditation

In addition to breathing exercises, I may use meditation as a way of preparing a client and myself for a session. We may take the first ten minutes of the session to meditate or breathe together to harmonize our energies and create more productive energy for our work together.

PROTECTING VITAL ENERGY PATTERNS

As indicated before, many people try to steal energy from others instead of trying to generate their own when they are feeling low in energy. Most clients who come to therapy tend to want to do that, so, as a therapist, if you don't know how to protect yourself from "professional energy stealers," you will burn out rather quickly. I am convinced that the ability to protect one's vital energy from energy stealers is an important skill for most people and absolutely essential for teachers, therapists, or anyone who works directly with other people.

Crucial to this skill is an awareness of your boundaries and the ability to protect those boundaries when someone is intruding on your space. This is partly behind the notion of giving each other space in a relationship.

When someone is stealing their energy, many people don't recognize it until it's too late. You have probably had the experience of talking to someone, and after they left, you felt drained and didn't know why. One of my favorite ways of helping people learn to recognize when they are letting someone steal their energy is the following structured exercise.

I ask clients to share a recent decision they have made that they feel good about. Then I ask them to pay attention to their reactions and what happens in their body while I deliberately try to talk them out of the decision. Frequently they try to defend their decision (energy down the drain), or they tighten their jaw or other parts of their body (e.g., the stomach; further energy down the drain), or they may withdraw by closing down their breathing, looking away, and the like (all activities that drain energy).

When this type of energy stealing occurs, the best response is to remain centered and let the intrusion either go by or take action to stop the intrusion. One of the concepts I teach my clients is how to restore a sense of connection with their own energy when situations like the structured one above happen in their lives. No one can remain above all such events. No one can remain centered all the time. The trick is to notice rather quickly that one is off center and then take some actions to get back on center again.

A rather new definition of health recognizes the issue of how quickly a person can return to a calm or relaxed state after being pulled out of that state as a result of some stress. This can be quantified by measuring such things as heart and pulse rate and then having the subject run in place for several minutes. Heart and pulse rates are checked repeatedly until they return to their pre-stress levels. The time required for this to happen is an indication of one's physical fitness level. The same is true with psychological fitness. Any argument or obsessive thoughts that persist keep a person off center longer.

SHARING CREATIVE ENERGY PATTERNS

One of the persistent problems that often brings people to therapy is an inability to share energy with others. Clients frequently feel cut off from others and don't seem to have any synergistic ways to exchange energy with others. I use group therapy most often with these people because it gives me and the client a living laboratory in which to practice the necessary skills. I can observe directly how the client goes about trying to make contact, and I can make specific suggestions and interventions to assist him or her.

One such client was an artist who had withdrawn into his art during adolescence to avoid making contact with others. He was an excellent artist, but his work was also his biggest problem because it served as an escape for him when he became fearful of sharing energy with someone. He actually believed that he could make himself invisible when he was around people — and thus avoid having to face his fears of closeness.

He wasn't in group long before this pattern began to show up and other group members began to react to his attempts to become invisible. This led to his making an agreement with the other group members that he would attempt to make contact with each one during the therapy session and then make a report near the end of the session and get feedback from other group members. Gradually he began to shine and open up in the group so that making contact with him was much easier.

Sometimes I do mirroring exercises with clients to promote energy sharing. I also use more subtle exercises like the "sticky hands." This involves two people standing facing each other with one wrist touching the opposite wrist of the other person. The two take turns, with one leading the movement while the other attempts to follow, always keeping their wrists in contact. After a while, if energy flows between them, they can do this with neither one leading nor following.

BALANCING ALL LIFE ENERGY PATTERNS

I spent some time studying the various energies and energy centers in the body, and out of my study I have gained an appreciation for the art of balancing all our energies. Many different energies flow through the body. Some, like sexual energy and the protective energy coming out of the adrenal stress reaction, are stronger and more dominant. Others, like the psychic energies and more spiritual connections, are softer and more subtle.

The most effective way I have found to understand and utilize these energies in balance is to use the *chakra* or energy centers as a grounding for my awareness.[3] The accompanying chart shows these centers and the kinds of energy that emanate from them. Each center can have too much energy or too little energy. The optimum condition is a balancing of all the energy in the body. Some people over-focus on their sexual or power energies and have little or no awareness of higher, more subtle energies. Others, through meditation and other spiritual practices, may have learned to make contact with their higher energies but have little or no grounding energy to counterbalance these other energies. These people may have trouble functioning in the everyday world.

The ways that I locate blocked or excessive energy at each of the chakras are numerous and often involve intuitive processes. One simple way is to do a body reading, which can tell much and give clues to follow up on through other methods. For example,

---

3. The term *chakra* and the system of energy centers in the body are taken from Hindu philosophy and medicine. Reference to energy centers in the body is also found in ancient Hebrew, Buddhist and Chinese cultures.

CHAKRAL ENERGY CENTERS

Crown Chakra
Center of cosmic consciousness and unconditional enlightenment. Liberation from limits of mind and body realities. Blissful unity with pure and universal energy beyond all dualities.

Throat Chakra
Center of creativity, self-expression, and intuition for higher consciousness and communication. Influences inspiration and repression.

Spleen Chakra
Center of sexual and reproductive energy. Energy can be used for cleansing, purification, and health. Balances the opposing energies of anxiety and well-being.

Brow Chakra (Third Eye)
Source of ecstasy, ESP, clairvoyance, and christ consciousness. Integrative thought and wisdom. Visionary powers. Heightened self-awareness.

Heart Chakra
Center of unconditional love and compassion. Energy helps create immunity to disease. Dominant emotions are joy and grief. Gateway to higher consciousness and more subtle energy.

Solar Plexus Chakra
Center of power and emotional energy. Center of opposites or polarities (control or be controlled, powerful or powerless). Influences ego strength and conditional love.

Root Chakra
Being grounded. Pleasure center for the body. Concerned with basic existence and survival. Influences sexual activity, regeneration, and creativity. This energy can enhance personal growth, health, healing, intuition, and intelligence, or it can create an over-concern for safety and survival.

7

6

5

4

3

2

1

physical groundedness (root chakra) is easy to check. Ask the client to stand relaxed, as he or she might usually stand. Then push the person slightly from the front, back, and both sides. Some people will attempt to stay where they are and resist you, trying to remain grounded. Others will simply move with you and ground themselves in the spot they moved to, while others who have little or no physical grounding could literally be pushed across the room.

This activity can tell me whether the person is too grounded and has considerable energy tied up in security and survival issues. Such people are highly resistant to change and generally work slowly in therapy. The ungrounded person, in contrast, is likely to bounce off the walls when he or she starts to change, and may need additional help to stay grounded.

Sexual energy (spleen chakra) can be assessed by the way people walk and how they carry themselves. If their pelvis is tilted forward when they walk or just stand, this is an indication of strong sexual energy. On the other hand, a pelvis that is tilted back to protect the genital area may be an indication of repressed or low sexual energy.

The third (or so-called power) chakra can be detected by upper body posture and build. People who slump over slightly and have rather shallow breathing are usually closing down the power chakra, which is located behind the solar plexus. Heavy upper body build could indicate excessive energy devoted to power and control of self and others.

The heart chakra energy can also be detected by breathing and body posture. Shallow breathing in the upper lobes of the lungs and a shallow inhale would indicate some blockage. Rounded shoulders and caved-in chest are also indicators of blocked energy. Open, over-expanded upper body with strong inhale could be an indication of too much heart energy not in balance with other energies.

The throat is the center of the fifth chakra. Listening to the quality of sounds made during normal speech can provide some clues. A light, high-pitched voice can indicate tension and blockage, for example. Listening to and watching breathing patterns can also yield much information about the energy at this chakra. The throat has to open to allow free passage of air to the lungs as we breathe. By observing how easily this occurs, you can assess the energy levels. The throat chakra also controls verbal communication and expression of the other energies. If it is too open, the expression is often scattered and confusing. Such people talk too fast and often don't know what they are expressing. Hesitant and halting speech patterns may indicate low energy in this chakra.

The energy of the third eye is usually more subtle and harder to read through observation. Generally I look for the degree of self-awareness and how that is balanced with the awareness of others. Too much focus on self might indicate excessive energy, while too much concern for what others think and do can indicate blocked energy.

The crown chakra energies are detectable by holding your hand palm down six to eight inches above a person's head. The stronger the energy, the more tingling you will feel in the palm of your hand. This energy may be weak in some people and undetectable until the blocks at the lower chakras are removed.

Energy Balancing Techniques

After I have assessed where energy is out of balance either by being blocked or being too strong, I begin to use various energy balancing tools. In this work it is useful to have a wide variety of therapy tools. The therapy tools used in the psychodynamic, behavioristic, and humanistic schools are most helpful in dealing with imbalances involving the first three chakras. The higher chakras are served best by more spiritual, meditative, and non-Western therapy tools.

Quite often I use breathing as a basic energy balancing tool. Upon locating blocked energy centers, I can have the client breathe into those areas and learn to release the blocked energy. Placement of the breath is a way to focus energy. In addition, I sometimes use a small, hollow, rubber or plastic play ball (four to five inches in diameter); by having the client place it on the spine at the point of blocked energy and having him or her breathe into that area, a release occurs quite quickly.

Bioenergetic exercises and stress postures are often useful to increase the tension and force a rebound release in the muscles that may have contracted around a blocked energy center. I sometimes have clients kneel and slam a tennis racket on a pillow. I have them grip the racket with both hands and swing it back over their heads as far as they can, then slam it down, making a sound. This often opens up the third chakra and enables clients to make contact with their feelings. Gestalt and Neurolinguistic Programming (NLP) work on polarities is helpful in dealing with blocked third chakra energy.

Breathing is also useful for contacting the higher, more subtle energies. Too, I use guided imagery, meditation, and movement activities to deal with blocks at the higher centers.

Alignment of Energy in Relationships

An area that I have just begun to explore is the alignment of the chakral energies between partners in a relationship. This alignment at all energy centers seems extremely important but not well understood. I have often heard couples say, "When he (she) didn't understand, I felt betrayed by him (her)." The word *betrayed* reflects being out of alignment with someone or having done something to break an alignment that previously existed.

The obvious example of betrayal in relationships is having sexual intercourse with someone other than the person with whom you are in alignment by being married, living together, or some other agreement. This same betrayal can occur at any of the other energy centers. Verbally sharing intimate thoughts and feelings with someone other than a partner in a committed relationship can be felt by the partner as a betrayal of the alignment at the throat chakra. By trying to exercise power and control over the thoughts or behavior of a partner, one may be betraying the alignment of the third chakra.

To promote alignment of energies, I introduce an exercise to enable the partners to spot areas in which misalignment is possible. They utilize the chart on page 100.

Step 1. Have both partners fill out the accompanying chart, rating self and partner on the perceived level of chakral energy (high, medium, or low) at each of the energy centers.

Step 2. Have the partners compare the ratings of each other, without trying to determine who is right or wrong if the perceptions disagree. The purpose is mostly to enable each to learn more

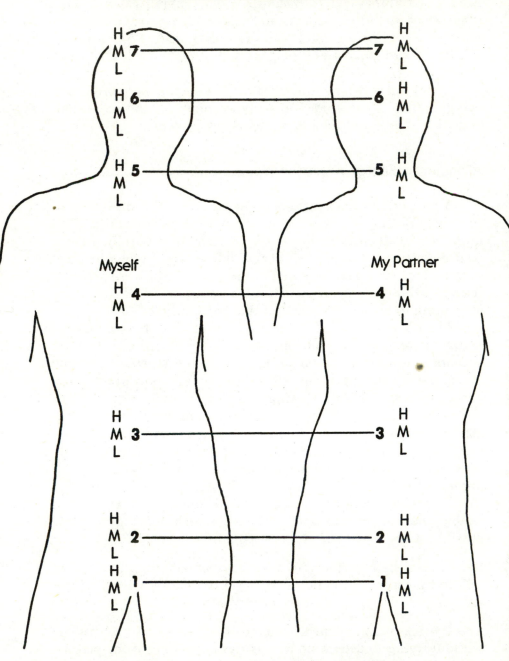

Myself

My Partner

about the other's perceptions. They should note where they have about the same level of energy and where there appears to be a discrepancy.

Step 3. Have the partners look at areas in which both noticed a discrepancy. For example, one partner may see himself or herself as low in sexual energy and the other may see this the same way, while both might agree that the other person is high in sexual energy. These perceptions point to possible areas in which betrayal might occur, indicating a direction for therapy or problem solving.

In another activity to promote the awareness of alignment of energies at each chakra, I have partners sit facing each other, eyes closed, holding hands. I give the following instructions:

1. Imagine a white light starting at the base of your spine. Breathe into that area.
2. Visualize the light beaming out toward your partner's root chakra.
3. Make an energy contact between you and your partner. (Pause 30 seconds.) Now say *LAH* and see if you can feel the vibrations at the base of your spine.
4. Move the white light up to your navel, and again visualize the beam of light extending out to your partner's second chakra. Make contact and hold that contact. (Pause 30 seconds.) Now say *BAH* and vibrate the sound into your second chakra. Notice any thoughts or feelings that come up for you while doing this.
5. Move the white light up to your solar plexus — the hole in the center of your upper abdomen just below the rib cage. Make contact with your partner, and again notice any thoughts or feelings. (Pause 30 seconds.) Now say *RAH* and vibrate into your third chakra.
6. Move the white light to the fourth chakra, in the middle of your chest. Make contact with your partner. Feel this area opening up to receive energy from your partner. Watch your thoughts and feelings emerge and dissolve. (Pause 30 seconds.) Now say *YM* (Ya-Mm) and allow the sound to fill your upper chest.

7. Move the white light to your throat just behind your larynx. Visualize the contact with your partner and notice your thoughts and feelings. (Pause 30 seconds.) Now make the sound *HAH* and vibrate your throat.

8. Move the white light to your third eye. Feel the contact with your partner. (Pause 30 seconds.) Make the sound *AH*. Feel it coming from your third eye.

   Optional: Open your eyes slowly and focus your attention on a single point in the middle of your partner's forehead. Let that one point become figure while everything else fades into the background. (Pause 5 minutes.) Close your eyes again.

9. Finally, move the white light to the top of your head. See/feel the contact with your partner and notice your thoughts and feelings (Pause 30 seconds.) Say *OM* several times and feel the energy releasing off the top of your head.

   Optional: Open your eyes, keeping them very soft. Focus your attention to a point several inches above your partner's head. (Pause 30 seconds.) Just focus and empty your mind of thoughts. See and feel the energy emanating from your partner's crown energy chakra.

10. Stay in eye contact with your partner and experience the openness that now exists between you.

At present, the practical uses of chakral energy awareness require much more study and experimentation. The activities in this chapter are designed to give you suggestions for beginning that exploration. I am cautious about drawing any definite conclusions from these activities, at the same time encouraging couples to allow any meaning to flow from their experiences.

7

A Transpersonal Approach to Working with Feelings

Gay Hendricks

As I think of what the most important issues are in being effective as a therapist, so many of them relate to how to deal with *feelings*. Learning to deal with feelings — my own as well as my clients' — was my first major step in becoming a transpersonal therapist. I would like to describe the moment at which I learned how to relate to my feelings in a liberating way, because it bears much on what I have to say in this chapter.

A REVELATION

One autumn day in the early 1970s, I was taking a walk in the Colorado Rockies. I had been wrestling with a number of difficult issues in my life. I was at a juncture in my personal life — I had just moved from California to take a new job — and I felt at a crisis point professionally. I had done all the things I was supposed to do to become an expert in my field, and I still did not feel like I knew anything that resonated deeply in my own heart about what brings about change in ourselves. I had learned a thousand facts and techniques, but none that I had personally discovered to be true about life and transformation. I was looking for the central problem, the one thing that made life difficult, the one thing we needed to do or not do to smooth out all of life. I had not found it.

On my walk I paused to consider these things, and I realized I had been looking outside myself for the answer to these questions. I had chased around the country seeking books, professors, and gurus, and it had not occurred to me to ask *myself* these questions. Until that moment, I had not been willing to trust my own experience.

So I asked myself what I most wanted to know for myself and my clients. How can I stop seemingly uninvited feelings from recycling through me over and over again? What can I do on a moment-to-moment basis that will enable me to let go of the past and greet each moment anew? How can I turn each moment, even the dreary ones, into an opportunity for spiritual and psychological growth? How do I get some quiet in my mind?

Within seconds the answers began sweeping through me in a way I had not expected. Instead of being logical thoughts, the answers came in the form of rushes of electric-like energy that seemed to leave the answers behind in their wake. This stunned me. I had not expected to receive answers in the form of an *experience*. The answers themselves were equally amazing to me because they spelled out an entirely different way of thinking. I would now characterize it as thinking with my body as well as my mind.

To the question of how to stop feelings from recycling through me over and over, the answer, experienced in my body, was: "Let yourself feel them completely." The feelings had recycled because I had not let myself experience them completely. Instead, my mind had tried to talk me out of them, to resist or ignore them. It was a revelation to me that a negative experience, such as anger or fear, could be dissolved by allowing myself to experience it. What had kept my negative feelings recycling was my own unwillingness to experience them!

This remarkable (to me) answer spilled over as part of the answers to the next question. I realized that I had held onto the past because I was resisting what I was experiencing in the present. I would, for example, replay tapes in my mind of an argument from the day before because I was unwilling to get in touch with the anger I was feeling right now in the present moment.

I saw that the glue that keeps us attached to the past is our resistance. We resist what is going on right now in ourselves and others, and it binds us tightly to old ways of being. I realized that at the bottom of all our problems was our resistance to love. When we resist our love for ourselves and others, we create endless dramas in our lives. When we drop our resistance, we open up space to love ourselves for who we are. By doing this, we also can love others for who they are.

I saw also that the way to peace of mind is through total participation in the present moment. Until we become willing to experience the truth of the present, our minds must restlessly ruminate about the past and the future. At the moment we become willing to see, feel, and hear what is *right now*, the mind becomes quiet and attentive. Meditation and other practices can help, but our willingness to experience the present is what brings about the moment-to-moment peace we seek.

These realizations led me to a totally new way of living my life and to a different way of practicing therapy. The day after I had the experience of these things, I saw a client who was deeply afraid. Instead of trying to talk her out of her feelings, I invited her to surrender to them fully. She underwent a deep experience of shaking and sobbing, followed by a period of quiet. In this period of quiet, several solutions to her problems appeared spontaneously to her.

I had heard the proverb, "The answer lies within," a number of times, but I had not seen it unfold before my eyes so dramatically. Here was a person who had moved from a state of confusion to a state of clarity by dropping her resistance and experiencing what she was experiencing. I was moved. Now, though I have since seen the same process a thousand times, I continue to be moved by the ability of people to discover their inner wellspring of creativity by becoming willing to experience how they are feeling right now.

BASIC ISSUES OF FEELING

Several basic issues are involved in learning to work with feelings. Among these are learning how to greet our feelings, learning how to express feelings, and learning how to greet the world so that it does not trigger unwanted feelings in us.

Learning to Greet Feelings in an Effective Way

Feelings are a natural human heritage. Our feelings themselves are not the problem, but our ways of greeting and handling those feelings often are.

It is commonly acknowledged that there are only a handful of basic feelings, such as fear, anger, sadness, happiness. If we greet those feelings with acceptance and if we express them clearly, they do not cause problems for us. Only when our strategies for experiencing and expressing our feelings are faulty do we have difficulty with them. Clients do not consult therapists because they are scared or angry but, rather, because they do not know effective strategies for relating to fear and anger or for expressing them.

How, then, do we relate most effectively to feelings? Early in life many of us experience a split between emotion and reason so that these two aspects of ourselves are in conflict rather than harmony. The mind, since it is the repository of our history of conditioning in regard to feelings, frequently tries to talk you out of the very feelings you most need to feel. To relate effectively with feelings, it is necessary to develop mental strategies that enable one to greet feelings with acceptance rather than resistance.

Rather than resisting our inner experience, we must greet it warmly. Rather than hating the way we feel about things, we must open up to those feelings, explore them, and ultimately come to love them.

Because of childhood conditioning, we frequently come to a confusing conclusion regarding whether our feelings are appropriate. Parents, in their zeal to have us be able to interact well with the outside world, want very much to get us to express only certain feelings, and those only in socially appropriate ways. Parents confuse expression with experience, so that we think something is wrong with our feelings themselves. The message that parents fail to give is: Your feelings are okay, but how you express them has to be fine-tuned. In regard to certain feelings, such as anger and sexuality, strong, confusing messages can be implanted, and these can later be uprooted only with great effort.

For example, parents do not want their children to express their sexuality in ways that have negative consequences. In building a strong taboo to prevent this, parents frequently communicate that something is wrong with sexual feelings themselves. This sort of message puts children in an intolerable bind, because to make it in the social environment, they must feel bad about something that feels good (albeit strange and confusing) to their organisms.

Thus, it is left to those in the helping professions to tell people that their feelings are perfectly all right but that they must learn effective ways of expressing those feelings so that positive consequences result for all.

Part of learning to relate to our feelings is to be willing to feel them deeply and completely. To use a metaphor from theater — when we deny feelings entirely, life becomes a tragedy. We die to our own inner experiences; life loses meaning; we cannot respond to others; illness and misery ensue. When we do not feel our feelings completely and deeply, life becomes a soap opera, full of recycling melodrama in the form of incomplete communications, silent suffering, untold truth, tawdry conspiracies, and other staples of afternoon TV.

What are we afraid of? Why do we mute our feelings so that we feel them only superficially? It seems that in the conditioning process we incorporate inaccurate beliefs about our feelings, based on what people have told us and what we have seen them doing. Some common, unfortunate beliefs that I have picked up from clients over the years are:

If I let myself feel my anger fully,
I will explode.
If I let myself feel as sad as I feel,
I will never stop crying.
If I let myself feel scared,
I will not be a real man.
If I let myself feel as sexual as I feel,
I will become promiscuous and insatiabl·
If I let myself feel as depressed as I feel,
I will die.

Sometimes these types of beliefs can be dissolved by awareness. Often, though, we must experiment personally with allowing ourselves to experience each feeling so that we can know for certain that feeling it is all right. In the realm of our feelings, there is no substitute for certainty.

A personal experience confirmed for me the point of view I have just expressed. Once, during a period of solitude in a cabin in the mountains, I began to experience boredom. Rather than submitting to the boredom and looking for something new to do, I began to experience it. Soon it dissolved and I got to the deeper feeling beneath it, which was a fear of being alone. This is truly one of the most primal of human feelings. I began to let myself experience it, feeling as if I were lowering myself into a maelstrom of unexplored stuff. For several hours I kept at it, feeling the sensations of the fear in my body, losing it, then getting back to it again.

Suddenly I burst through to the deepest experience of fear I had ever encountered. I began shaking and shuddering uncontrollably. I put on some music and began to dance, to have some outlet for the vibrations that were pouring through me. I kept dancing and experiencing the fear, with the intention of letting myself feel it to completion. Then, without warning, the fear dissolved and was replaced by a warm sense of quiet joy, which persisted for days afterward. Now, after many similar experiences, I know for certain in my body that all I need to do when I feel fear is to let myself experience it deeply.

As therapists, one of the most life-enhancing messages we can communicate to our clients is that at the bottom of all our feelings there is peace, bliss, and a deeper, more creative relationship with ourselves.

Learning to Express Feelings Effectively

In my own work with clients over the past decade, I have been most interested in finding what types of communication allow people to get off of recycling patterns on which they are stuck. For instance, a couple may be stuck on a pattern in which they argue about who is right and who is wrong. The pattern may repeat itself in a thousand intricate variations on the same theme. Is there a certain style or mode of communication that will stop these patterns and get to the resolvable issues at the bottom?

To use another example, let's say a woman has a recycling pattern of conflicts with her mother. What depth or intensity of communication is required to get away from the old pattern and come to a clear, possibly satisfying resolution? Asking these kinds of questions has led me to some ideas about what brings about a type of communication that dissolves problems rather than perpetuates them.

Most of us are afraid of communicating clearly. The reasons are simple. When we told the truth early in life, we got in trouble. Also, we saw people around us couching the truth in crooked terms. Generally, people do not do this maliciously. These mistakes are simply symptoms of a vast area of human unconsciousness and lack of skill in communication. Although we get twelve years of grammar and math in school, how much time is spent teaching us how to get in touch with our feelings and communicate them clearly? Acknowledging that most of us are first graders in the art of communicating clearly about our inner experience, what are the essential lessons about communication that need to be delivered to our clients?

Learning How to Greet the World Effectively ⎯⎯⎯⎯⎯⎯⎯

Problems clear up when one or more parties expresses a deeper level of feeling. I have witnessed the following scene many times: Two people are locked in an argument. They recycle the issues over and over. Nothing happens — no resolution, no agreement. Then one persons risks a deeper level of communication. The person says, "I'm angry about . . ." or, "I'm scared that . . ." or, "I need this from you." Something shifts, and the situation moves toward resolution. It is as if the entire argument rested on a deep feeling that had not been expressed. When finally expressed, the situation could clear up.

Deep expressions of feeling almost always begin with *I*, as in *I* am scared, *I'm* angry, *I* need, *I* want, *I'm* hurt. And the clearest communications seem to require the fewest words. People unknowingly try to make statements of feeling more complicated than they actually are, but the greatest movement occurs when one or more of the people in the situation is willing to risk being simple and to speak clearly, economically, from the heart.

Frequently in counseling I ask clients to look me in the eye and tell me the deepest level of feelings they are experiencing. I may give them examples of what the deepest feelings are, or I may ask questions designed to get them to tell me what they are scared, angry, or sad about. Not until the words actually come out of their mouths, though, does the real movement take place.

There seems to be something liberating about speaking the deepest truth about ourselves in the simplest possible terms.

People need to learn to take responsibility for their feelings. Blaming others for our feelings and our problems is one of the greatest barriers to effective living. Most people who consult counselors, however, are not prepared yet to assume full responsibility for their own experience, so counselors must first begin with people where they are. Only when people have had their point of view acknowledged do they become willing to move off it to a position of greater responsibility.

I find myself going through several stages in helping clients get to a place of responsibility in regard to an issue. Frequently I begin by listening carefully to the client's present point of view. For example, a man complains that his wife does not understand him. We explore how he feels when he is not understood, and we discuss recent examples of the problem.

When I feel he has had a chance to express his position clearly, I begin the second stage by introducing the idea that it is *his* issue, that he may want to consider that he is using the present situation with his wife to work out some past issue. I ask him if the present situation reminds him of anything from the past.

Then the third stage begins, in which we look at any past issues or any present resistance to taking full responsibility. Some people become upset at the concept that they are totally responsible for their lives, so we have to work on that before we can go further. In the case I am referring to, the man quickly saw that his present issue with his wife was actually a replay of an old issue with his mother. His mother was one of those people who needed to be right all the time, and his feeling of being wrong and misunderstood dominated his childhood. When he saw he was replaying that issue with his wife, he relaxed and was able to ask his wife clearly for what he wanted. As if by magic, she started listening to him in ways that he liked better.

Not all present problems refer back to an earlier problem, of course, and a person need not necessarily find the historical roots of a situation. All that is required, I have found, is that clients be *willing* to consider that the present issue is something of their own creation.

Something about the act of being willing to take responsibility frees up energy that moves the present situation to a new place.

Clarifying Intentions

In working with clients on their ability to communicate their feelings, I find a great deal of attention going into helping them get their intentions clear. So often in communicating, our intention is something other than communicating clearly. We let a past issue interfere with our ability to communicate the information we want to say in the present.

For example, a woman may want to tell her husband that she needs a few days to herself to meditate and be alone. Suppose that her intention is muddled by a belief she has that she can never get what she wants from men. She has a whole history of experiences that confirm this point of view. If her intention is not clear, she may pick a time or circumstance that does not favor his listening to her. She may tell him when he's upset, or in a place that does not support a dialogue on the subject. She may tell him in a tone of voice that triggers an argument rather than an effortless resolution. She may tell him in a way that activates a fear that she is going to leave him.

Many times I have asked clients (and myself) questions like:

What are your intentions in communicating this information?
Is it to make the other person wrong?
Is it to prove some belief you have about the world? (e.g., "See, I told you I can't get what I want from men!")
Can you present the information simply in a way that gets positive results?

Clarifying intention is in itself a valuable activity, because it gives clients an opportunity to examine their way of acting upon the world in getting their needs met. The results of communicating with clear intentions are often quickly manifested and readily apparent.

Fine-Tuning the Mind

If you have ever driven a car in which the front wheels are out of alignment, you know what an unpleasant vibration can result from such a small needed adjustment. In the same vein, the smoothness of our clients' trips down the road of life can be enhanced by relatively small adjustments in their style of thinking. Certain mental maladjustments can result in a rough trip. For this reason, I give considerable attention to helping clients look at their beliefs, to find out if their minds are serving them or enslaving them.

It is an odd paradox that the same mind that can write symphonies, cure polio, and build bridges can also make us miserable, sick, and commit suicide. The big brain of the human can use its awesome power for great leaps of liberation and imagination, and it can turn on itself and others with acts of oppression and destruction. At the center of the problem is the mind's tendency to generalize and form beliefs.

Some beliefs are formed under stress, when our minds are casting about in a storm for some mooring to hang on to. Others are the result of deliberate or unconscious inculcation at the hands of the people around us as we are developing. For example, a man could get the belief that "people can't be trusted" from being abandoned himself or from hearing that belief from his grandfather, who heard it from *his* grandfather. Regardless of the source of beliefs, they seem to generate unpleasant feelings far out of proportion to their size. One of the most satisfying aspects of working with beliefs in therapy is that I have often found clients able to make enormous changes in how they feel by clearing up even one inaccurate belief.

Here are some beliefs I have seen clients uncover which, when dissolved, significantly enhanced their feelings about themselves:

I am unlovable.
The world is an unsafe place.
In a conflict, I must always lose.
Nobody can be trusted.
If I go out into the world, I'll get in trouble.
I shouldn't be too successful.
I have to let boys be smarter and win.
If I can't get ahead, at least I can get revenge.

These are all examples of inaccurate views of reality. It is helpful to know that, since beliefs are made only by mindstuff, they do not actually exist. They are illusions and can be changed quickly through awareness and accurate information.

Asking clients to examine their beliefs, to see whether they hold mental positions that generate unpleasant feelings, has a powerful effect. First, the process uncovers areas in which the mind is being used against itself. And second, the very act of examining beliefs empowers clients by letting them know that the same mind that has been strong enough to limit their freedom and cause pain is also powerful enough to transform itself, liberating untold energy and creativity.

A Transpersonal Approach to Relationship Therapy

Barry Weinhold

Based upon my experiences as a practicing counselor and psychologist for the past twenty years, I would say that the most important and most frequent therapeutic issue that clients bring to therapy is a relationship problem. This is either in the form of a dysfunctional relationship or in trouble starting and keeping effective relationships.

Over the years I have used a variety of approaches to help clients achieve better, more satisfying relationships. Some have worked quite well and others not as well. I still search constantly for new and better ways of helping people deal with relationship problems. I have chosen to label what I do currently as a "transpersonal approach to relationship therapy." I use the word *transpersonal* because it incorporates and integrates every other approach I have used previously, and it is the largest context for dealing with relationships that I can effectively utilize for now. If you were to talk to me in another year, I may be doing the same things and I may not. It is an open system and cannot ever be seen as THE transpersonal approach either by others or by myself.

THE BASIS FOR TRANSPERSONAL RELATIONSHIP THERAPY ⎯⎯⎯⎯

As a therapist, I see that my clients are stuck because they have faulty and limited views of themselves, other people, and the world. My job is first to help them recognize their misperceptions and the negative, limited effects these misperceptions are having currently in their lives. Then my work focuses on helping them develop a more expansive (transpersonal) view of themselves, other people, and the world. I finally help them "ground" these views in the reality of their day-to-day world. In this approach, the world or other people need not change. But the clients must change their views of themselves in relationship to other people and the world in more expansive ways. In doing this, they learn a requisite variety of ways to lead happier, more socially useful, productive lives.

The underlying assumptions I use in working with people are as follows:

1. You were born feeling okay about yourself. If you are now feeling not okay in some important ways, you had to have learned these feelings from your relationships with others.

2. At birth you were connected to the transpersonal, the universal source of love. This connection, however, is fragile and must be nurtured until you are able to maintain that transpersonal connection for yourself. If this connection is not nurtured by conscious parenting — and in most cases I see, it was not, you will literally forget who you are and develop instead an image of who you are that is more in line with the prevailing social and psychological norms of your family of origin.

3. All relationships with others are a reflection of your relationship with yourself. You project into your relationships all the issues you haven't solved with yourself.

4. Anything unresolved in your relationship with your parents and other members of your family of origin will show up in your current relationships. This original set of relationships seems to set the pattern for your relationships with yourself and others.

5. You are never upset for the reason you think you are. Our current perceptions are limited to and are colored by unresolved issues from the past.

6. Forgiveness, which means to give back, is the major means of changing your misperceptions. In the process of remembering who you really are, you will need to give back to others those thoughts, perceptions, beliefs, and values you took from them as ways of defining who you are.

7. You cannot change the world you live in or other people, but you can change your perceptions of the world, of other people, and of yourself.

8. The two core emotions are fear and love. All fears are based on some misperception. Anger, sadness, and guilt are emotions that keep you from your experience of fear and love. Any emotion, core or otherwise, that is not expressed fully will continue to rule your life.

9. You are what you believe you are. Your current beliefs are based on your perceptions of the past, which you relive over and over again in the present.

10. Because you forgot who you really are, you have trouble developing a clear picture of your psychological boundaries in relationship to others, particularly close relationships. As a result, you violate others' boundaries and are violated yourself, and you don't know how to deal with the effects of these violations.

RELATIONSHIP PATTERNS _____

Low Self-Esteem _____

> *Client Statement:* "I just don't like myself very much."

> *Problem:* Most people grow up thinking they must have done something wrong to have been so badly treated as a child. Clients typically ask themselves, "Why me?" or, "What did I do to deserve this?" When I ask clients what their bottom-line, most persistent, negative thought is about themselves, it almost always boils down to, "I'm not good enough" or, "I'm not enough" in some important ways. This usually follows a long history of self-blame and self-pity.

Sometimes this pattern is not obvious to the client *or* the therapist. To cover up their unlovable feelings, clients often try to maintain a facade of liking themselves. They over-identify with their "good" self and deny or repress any "bad" thoughts or feelings.

I generally assess my clients' self-esteem using four criteria: connectiveness, uniqueness, power, and identity. As they describe their problems, I try to determine in which of these four areas they need to work, and that is where I focus my attention.

Operating Principles

1. My job in connection with this pattern is to help clients see the misperceptions they have made and to help them understand the basis for forming those misperceptions. Essentially, I teach clients how they got the way they are. I ask them questions like, "How do you know who you really are?"

2. After they understand what has happened to produce this pattern, I teach them a process of changing their perceptions to bring their self-perceptions more in line with the way they really are.

3. After they have changed their perceptions and beliefs about themselves and realize how those changes are connected to new life experiences, they begin to identify increasingly with who they really are. They then start to behave more in accord with the new perceptions and less with the old ones.

Therapeutic Tools

I choose from a variety of tools, depending on the client's favorite way of representing his or her experiences to me. If the client is predominantly visual ("I *picture* all these other persons as better than me"), I might use visually oriented tools such as imagery or visualizations. For example, I might say, "See if you can remember a time when you really liked yourself. Tell me about it as if it were happening right now, and describe what you see happening and how you feel."

For auditory clients, I may ask for reports of the negative message they hear and ask them to do "thought listening" exercises and write down themes or actual words and phrases. With persons who are primarily kinesthetic, I might have them do breathing exercises to help them learn how to locate and expand loving feelings in their body or teach them how to release fearful feelings stored in their body.

Therapeutic Tool #1: Use of Permissions.[1] People who have essentially believed that they are not worth much often have to be given permission to believe otherwise. I use several methods to give permissions, always working toward the goal of helping these clients learn how to give themselves the permissions they need. One especially helpful tool I have found is to have clients read the following list of high impact permissions, pausing (indicated by §) after each one to determine any resistances that they are aware of. This activity combines the visual, auditory, and kinesthetic senses. I ask clients to pay attention to their thoughts, feelings, and body sensations (breathing changes, heart beat, rushes of energy, sinking feelings, etc.).

---

1. From Barry Weinhold and Gail Andresen, *Threads: Unraveling the Mysteries of Adult Life* (New York: Richard Marek Publishers, 1979).

I, _____, deserve love. □ I now realize that I am in truth a radiantly beautiful cosmic miracle, aglow with love and light. □ I deserve love and respect just for being alive. □ Love and creativity flow through me freely to everyone in the world and return again to me. □ My own loving nature makes it easy for me to forgive every offense against me and every mistake from which I suffered. □ I forgive myself for all my mistakes and offenses against myself. □ I forgive my mother for all her mistakes and offenses, and I acknowledge her love for me and mine for her. □ I forgive my father for all his mistakes and offenses, and I acknowledge his love for me and mine for him. I now give and receive love freely. □ I am an open channel for the expression of love and creativity in great abundance. □ I can best fulfill my Self by being my own loving, creative Self in my own way, doing what I choose, always coming from my own center. □ I alone create my life and destiny. □ I accept that responsibility and now declare that I have let go of the illusion that anyone else's decisions have power over me without my full agreement. □ All my thoughts, words, and deeds are creative, powerful. □ It is safe for me to love and trust people and to let myself accept the love and trust that is my birthright. □ I have given up pretending that anyone can hurt me without my permission. □ I see good will in everyone. □ I realize that I am connected to and loved by everyone who is important to me. □ I am now willing to let go of all the negative, life-denying thought structures that I programmed myself with at birth. □ I'm glad I was born. □ I have the right to be here. □ I deserve love. □ I deserve love just for being alive. And I know that, in truth, all there is . . . is love.

As clients are reading the list, I record on my list those statements that seem to generate the most resistances. I may ask the client to prioritize the list, from most resistance to least, and then we work with several of the most resistant ones. I give clients homework assignments, asking them to write these statements repeatedly several times a day, along with responses to them, and to bring what they have written to the next session.

For example, if a client would write, "I deserve love and respect just for being alive" and if the self-response would be something like, "No, I have to earn it," I would help this person write another permission intended to gently dislodge that resistance. One such permission could be, "I have earned the right to love and respect by being born," or some other permission that incorporates the resistance as part of the statement, thus creating a larger context for the permission. Since all resistance is seen as the result of limited perceptions, a way to dislodge resistance is to incorporate it into a larger context.

Judy, a 26-year-old single female, came to me with a specific problem and a specific request. In the first session she said, "My life is going real well. I have a good job and I'm respected and loved by my friends and family, but I can't seem to find any men I would consider forming a long-term relationship with. Will you help me with this?" My response was, "Well, I don't have any eligible men waiting in the next room to introduce you to, but let's look at what kind of man and relationship you're looking for. Describe in as much detail as you can the characteristics of the man and the relationship you want."

She replied quickly with a fairly long and complete list of characteristics of the kind of man and relationship she would like. So I asked her to write the following sentence: "I now am meeting and establishing the kind of relationship I want with men who are . . . (listing of characteristics)." I asked her to write that as many times as she wanted during the next week and to be prepared to discuss the results the following week when we were to meet again.

By the next session she reported meeting one man, at least, who matched her qualifications, and he would be taking her out this weekend. Before her third session she called me in somewhat of a panic and said, "I don't know what to do. I'm feeling overwhelmed because I've met two more men this week who meet my qualifications." My advice to her was to stop writing the statements and to enjoy the success she had reaped for herself! We talked again about how to manage this new prosperity in her life, but essentially her therapy on this issue was completed.

Therapeutic Tool #2: Use of Breathing. Frequently, people with low self-esteem are completely cut off from any good feelings in their body. Their thought patterns become overly identified with faults, mistakes, and shortcomings that they become obsessed with. I often use breathing exercises with these people to get them out of their head and into their body, where they can begin to make contact with themselves and learn to nurture themselves with their breathing. I teach them to connect their inhale and exhale to produce an equal exchange of air. This breathing pattern — pulling on inhale and letting go on exhale — allows them to begin to reconnect with feelings and sensations in their body.

First I ask them to focus all their attention on their breathing, and then I occasionally suggest that they pay attention to the feelings and sensations in their body. Often, sad, scared, or angry feelings come up, whereupon I ask them to merely notice the feelings and then return the focus to their breathing. When they are able to do this, they get a quick and often easy release of these feelings while they are breathing. They might experience physical release in the form of vibrating, shaking, or the sensation of a physical mass leaving their body while they remain calm and focused on their breathing. This is a wonderful way to release stored tension (dis-ease) from the body, and it also helps these people reconnect with core feelings of love, bliss, joy, and ecstasy.

Arthur was a 45-year-old real estate salesman who came to me because he had difficulty getting close to people. He felt unlovable and unworthy of a close, loving relationship. Even though he had been married for some time, he had not dealt with these feelings. Although his self-esteem seemed high in work-related areas, he did not feel good about himself in his marriage relationship. In my observing his body and his breathing, it became clear to me how cut off this man was from his body, and consequently from his feelings, both positive and negative.

I decided to teach him some breathing exercises to see if he could be taught to reconnect with his feelings. I moved slowly at first, giving him the sense that he was in charge of how fast we moved.

In his sixth session, while he was practicing his breathing exercise, things began to happen quickly. As he breathed, he began to identify a sensation of extreme tightness in the middle of his chest, which he identified as fear. I instructed him to make as complete contact with that feeling as he could and when he felt he had established that contact, to begin to spread that feeling out in all directions from its seeming origin in his chest. Slowly, with my instructions and reassurance, he began to allow the feeling to move down into his stomach and pelvis and up into his upper chest and shoulders. As he did that, his body began to shake noticeably — to which I issued more reassurance about how his body was opening up to the feeling and the shaking was all part of this process and nothing more. Soon he had spread the feelings throughout his body and was experiencing an intense release of fear. With my now fairly constant reassurance and permissions to continue breathing, the process ran its course and the vibrating and shaking in his body subsided. Then I asked him how he was feeling. He replied, "I feel great, full of energy, and the fear is gone."

After that, I asked him to return to his breathing and make contact with a feeling of love that he could identify in his body. Much to my surprise, he indicated that he felt intense love coming from the same place in his chest where he had felt intense fear just fifteen minutes before. I asked him to make strong contact with that feeling and to begin the same process of spreading it out in all directions from that area of his body. He did as I instructed and soon reported that his whole body was filled with the feelings of love. This time there was no shaking or vibrating — only a quiet hum accompanied by a wonderful smile and tears of joy streaming from his eyes. After some time in this state, he finally said to me, "I am whole again."

I pointed out to Arthur that whenever he might feel the fear sensations again, he now had a way he could use to diffuse the fear and release it. I advised him to use this tool whenever he needed it. I also asked him to practice his breathing regularly and let himself feel love throughout his body whenever he wanted to. In subsequent sessions he reported continued progress in opening up to his wife and experiencing a flow of love between them.

Poor Ego Boundaries and Limits

Client Statement: "I have a hard time being *me* in a relationship. I just seem to lose myself."

Problem: Many people I see in therapy have poorly established ego boundaries and have trouble setting effective limits for themselves and with others in relationships. The closer they get in a relationship, the more difficulty they have. They often express that they are afraid they will lose themselves if they get close, which prevents them from experiencing much genuine closeness at all in their relationships.

At another level, often they are helpless victims of verbally and physically intrusive partners and don't know how to cope with these repeated violations of their psychological space. We share the concept of territoriality with all other species on this planet. As human beings, we also have a psychological territory that consists of all our feelings, thoughts, behaviors, and our body. Because of our negative programming while growing up, we don't feel we can be responsible for all of our territory. We try to make others responsible for our feelings ("He made me angry"). We let others tell us what to think or do, and we abuse our body as if it didn't belong to us.

Operating Principles

1. With this kind of relationship pattern, you as a therapist should not intrude on the client's space without a clear

agreement or contract as to how and why and under what conditions you will do so. You should model for the client how to establish effective limits and boundaries in a therapeutic relationship. I spend considerable time establishing a therapy contract (usually written) that spells out the limits of the relationship and how those limits are going to be utilized in therapy. Consequences must be established as well, so that any violations of the time, process, role, and other limits are used to strengthen the boundaries.

2. Basically, with this pattern perhaps more than any other, I teach the clients in every way I can how to:
   a. identify their psychological territory;
   b. notice when their territory is being violated;
   c. communicate their limits effectively in a relationship;
   d. make effective agreements to share their territory; and
   e. expand their territory more and more to create the largest possible context for their relationship with themselves and others.

Relationship with the Client as a Therapeutic Tool

A description of more specific tools is prefaced by the reminder that the most important therapeutic tool remains your relationship with your client. Everything that happens in the relationship presents you with a rich source of data about how your clients set limits in relationships with themselves and others. This requires you to have your own well-developed relationship and limit-setting skills. To teach limit setting, I sometimes role play limit-setting situations that clients bring to therapy, often playing their part to model effective behavior. I might ask them to audiotape the therapy sessions and listen to or transcribe the session. This is useful to support the learning from the therapy session. I also give them step-by-step limit-setting processes to practice between sessions.

Therapeutic Tool #1: Intrusion. With clients who have a history of allowing intrusion without knowing it, I often contract with them to deliberately intrude on their psychological space. This is done

125

to help them develop an awareness of what feelings they are having that could serve as cues to let them know when someone is intruding on their space. One way is to ask clients to share a decision they made recently that they feel good about but in which there may be doubts. I then proceed to tell them and show them what a bad decision that was and deliberately try to bring out any doubts. As I do that, I ask them to pay attention to their thoughts and feelings so they can get a sense of what clues they may get when the intrusion is more subtle.

In the next session I have clients look for situations in which they are intruded upon and begin to notice their reactions. By having them bring these situations back to therapy, we can role play effective ways to handle them.

Therapeutic Tool #2: Limit Setting. Frequently, clients identify intrusive situations in which they don't know what to do. In these cases I teach clients a five-step communication process that, if used effectively, can help them learn to take care of their psychological territory and make effective agreements to share territory with another person. The more they respect the limits of others, the closer they can get to others. Although the steps, as outlined below, seem rather mechanical at first to most people, I find that they learn to integrate them into their personal style rather quickly:

1. Identify how you are *feeling*. Get in touch with the core feeling of fear. Some people use anger or sadness to cover their fears, so they should continue to look for any fears masked by anger or sadness. (Example: "I get scared when . . . .")
2. Describe the *behavior* that upsets you. Make the description as nonjudgmental as possible. (Example: "You change your plans at the last minute . . . .")
3. Tell the other person the *impact* of his or her behavior on you. The impact should be as tangible as possible. (Example: ". . . because now I have to change my plans, too, with only short notice.")
4. Make a *request* of the other person. This request should be in the form of a question. (Example: "Will you not change any plans that involve me at the last minute unless you have discussed it with me first and have my agreement on the changes?")

5. If the person says "no" to your request, *negotiate*. Ask, "What are you willing to agree to?"

Steps 1, 2, or 3 can be transposed, and often are. For instance, a person could say, "When you change your plans at the last minute, I have to change mine and I get scared that I can't count on you. Will you not change plans that involve me at the last minute unless you discuss it first with me and get my agreement?"

I usually have clients role play a problem or limit-setting situation with me during a session to help them learn these steps. When working with a couple, I have them go through the steps with each other in the session, with some coaching from me. On step 4 I often tell clients that the best way to make that step work for them is to (a) ask for what they want, (b) enjoy what they get, and (c) continue to work on any difference between the two.

Therapeutic Tool #3: Ground Rules for Making and Keeping Agreements. Many of the couples I work with are having difficulty making and keeping agreements with each other. Also, if they don't seem to have a way of handling broken agreements, I may present these as problem-solving tools to use when they are talking about a broken agreement. The ground rules are:

1. Make only agreements that you are sure you want to and are willing to keep.
2. Locate and communicate to your partner any potential broken agreements before they are broken. (Example: "I realize we left a loophole in our agreement, and I would like to close it before we have trouble.")
3. If you have broken an agreement, discuss this with your partner at the earliest appropriate time. (Example: "I just realized that I can't have dinner with you as I had planned because I forgot about a meeting I agreed to attend.")
4. Take responsibility for breaking an agreement, and discuss ways to make sure it doesn't happen again. Don't give excuses or justify your action. (Example: "I did break that agreement, and I would like to find a way to keep it from happening again.")

5. Find the other person right (instead of wrong) for what he or she is doing. (Example: "I can see why you didn't say anything to me.")

6. State the problem as you see it, always coming from your own experience, and ask your partner to do the same. (Example: "What I experienced was confusion about the agreement, and I didn't clear it up. What was your experience?")

7. Tell your partner what solution(s) you would like (Example: "What I would like is to start over with a new agreement.")

8. If you feel your partner is blaming you, ask whether he or she is willing to forgive you. If not, ask what is wanted from you before he or she is willing to forgive you. (Example: "Will you forgive me for breaking our agreement?" If the answer is "no," ask, "What do you want from me before you can forgive me?")

9. Be complete. Don't withhold things you think your partner may not like or may react defensively to. (Example: "I know you want me to change that, but I'm not willing to do it.")

I use one or more of these ground rules separately for clients who seem to have gaps in their awareness that one of the ground rules could fill, or I use them collectively as a framework for helping people make agreements and know how to handle breaches of those agreements. These ground rules often augment the five-step process mentioned above.

Recycled Developmental Issues

Client Statement: "I seem to have the same problems over and over again."

Problem: Any unresolved issue with one's parents while growing up will continue to recycle in current relationships until it is resolved.[2] The issue can

---

2. Ibid.

manifest in several predictable ways. First, people are likely to see the personality characteristics of one or both parents in present relationships. She says, "He has a temper just like my father," and he says, "She treats me just like my mother did." Usually these traits show up more in close relationships. Weinhold's rule (as I call it) is that the closer the relationship is, the more likely these unwanted characteristics are to show up in the partner, and in a form that will have the most detrimental effect on the relationship.

Another way this recycling process occurs is that people recreate the same relationship their parents had with them. For instance, if a man had trouble dealing with his mother's temper, he will probably attract someone who treats him in a similar way even though when he first met her, this dynamic was not obvious.

In addition, a person may attempt to recreate the same relationship his or her parents had with each other while he or she was growing up. The parents' relationship was the model, and probably the most familiar one. If the parents' relationship was conflictual, one will likely attract individuals who are conflict-prone and reject those who are easy to get along with.

Finally, people likely attract those whose patterns fit their patterns perfectly. If they have a pattern of people abandoning them during conflicts, for example, they will likely attract people whose biggest problem is running away from conflicts — even though the opposite seemed apparent upon first meeting.

I often tell clients that the people whom they have trouble dealing with in their lives are sent to them by "central casting" to help them learn how to deal with that particular issue. This usually brings a smile and a new way to look at difficult people.

Operating Principles

1. My first task is to help clients recognize that their upsets usually are not what they think they are but are the result of recycled childhood upsets and problems.

129

2. My second step is to help clients locate what the specific recycled issue actually is and help them understand the developmental problem involved.
3. This usually leads to the identification of these and other recycled issues in their present relationships.
4. Finally, I help clients develop a cooperative framework for handling recycled issues and upsets.

Written Processes, Neurolinguistic Programming, Breathing and Imagery Techniques as Therapeutic Tools

To help clients uncover the recycled issues and problems, I use a number of written processes. These are useful in enabling clients to increase their awareness and make connections with their childhood. In addition, I use some neurolinguistic programming tools to help people contextually reframe their problems and change their perceptions of what happened to them while they were growing up. Finally, I use breathing and imagery techniques to help clients get more in touch with their childhood feelings and memories that remain stored in their body.

Therapeutic Tool #1: Reframing Contexts. Very often clients come with unresolved issues that they are trying to get rid of. These issues cause them discomfort, and they would like to be free of their limiting effects. One of the first ways I help them to reframe their behavior is by asking them to think of as many positive reasons for having the unwanted behavior as they can. Then I ask them to take their list and reduce it to the two or three most likely positive purposes for that behavior. Finally, I ask them to come up with two or three new ways of achieving those same purposes without any adverse effects.

This process can take some time for clients who are attached to a belief that the behavior in question is bad and that they are bad for behaving this way. With such a person the reframing has to go through several additional steps, as follows:

1. Clients need to see that their behavior served them well to get through difficult times while they were growing up.

2. They need to understand that their parents and others were doing destructive things to them and that their now unwanted behavior helped them cope with the situations. Time must be allowed to help them locate and express their anger as they fully realize how badly they were treated.

3. Next, clients need to realize that even though their parents were doing these things and are responsible for doing them, they are not guilty. I often ask a client, "If someone else had been born into your family instead of you at the time you were born, would your parents have treated that person the same way they did you?" If the answer is "yes," I tell them, "Don't take what happened so personally." This often helps clients begin to overcome the "why me?" syndrome that can lead to self-pity.

   One client said to me after thinking about that statement for over a month, "You know, the more I thought about that statement, the better I felt. I guess I was still holding on to some thought that I did something wrong to cause my parents to mistreat me. Now I know that isn't true and anyone would have gotten the same treatment."

4. Generally when clients reach this point, having dealt with their feelings, they can begin to reframe their own behavior and reframe their perceptions of their parents and their whole childhood.

Therapeutic Tool #2: Expanding Contexts. Frequently the context for dealing with a relationship problem is too small or narrow, so the major therapeutic intervention involves helping the client develop a broader framework for dealing with the problem. This is apparent in the following case example.

A man and woman came to get help with a sexual problem. The problem was that whenever he initiated sexual contact, she would have a panic reaction because of old memories of how her father had made inappropriate sexual advances. As a result of the panic reaction, she would turn off sexually and he would be sexually frustrated and get scared that something was wrong with him sexually. He was very upset because these problems began to show up only after they had made a commitment to be sexually monogamous with each other.

131

In talking with the man, I realized that his definition or context was that unwanted problems were keeping the two of them from being close. What I suggested instead was that he view the cooperative problem-solving process as just another way to be close and not something to keep them from closeness. His response to this suggestion was overwhelmingly positive, and it provided an expanded context for the couple to work out ways to deal with the panic response.

Therapeutic Tool #3: Building a Cooperative Framework For Handling Upsets. In my experience, the ingredient that differentiates successful and unsuccessful relationships is that in successful relationships the couple has worked out an effective way of handling upsets. Successful relationships probably have just as many issues and problems as unsuccessful ones, but the difference is that upsets are handled and resolved quickly and completely.

The general context for successful relationships is that both partners ask for what they want, are satisfied with what they get, and continue to work on any differences until they are resolved. Conversely, in an unsuccessful relationship the partners do not ask for what they want, are not satisfied with what they get, and are unwilling to work on any differences.

An effective cooperative framework has to have some of the following ingredients:[3]

1. There must be an agreement that resolving problems is a form of intimacy and therefore takes precedence over other activities. Thus, the commitment is that both parties are willing to do what is necessary, including enduring some discomfort and sacrifice, to resolve conflicts and solve problems. Operationally, this means agreeing to stop whatever they are doing when an upset occurs and dealing with it before moving on. If that isn't possible, they need to make an agreement to deal with the upset at the next available time.

---

3. These have been taken from Gail Andresen and Barry Weinhold, *Connective Bargaining: Communicating About Sex* (Englewood Cliffs, NJ: Prentice-Hall, 1981).

2. Since conflicts or upsets aren't always what they appear to be at first, both persons must be committed to looking for deeper core issues, generally relating to unresolved childhood issues with parents. All problems are seen as opportunities to learn whatever lesson hasn't been learned. The only two real conditions that exist in a relationship are opportunities to learn lessons and bliss. All other conditions are the result of mistaken beliefs or perceptions. This part of the relationship process may involve being willing to help each other get to the underlying lessons by listening and giving feedback. It also involves being able to see that when the partner is upset, he or she is indirectly saying, "I need help; I don't know what to do."

3. The cooperative framework entails an agreement to share upsets and issues with each other and not try to solve them alone.

4. Neither party engages in negative forecasting, or worrying about problems that have not yet appeared. This is likely to create more problems than it solves.

5. Both agree to learn and use effective, straight communication skills with each other. I usually give clients a handout with effective communication rules and instructions on how to practice them. A copy of these rules ("Basic Guidelines for Communication") is included in the Appendix to this book.

6. The partners agree that nothing will ever be taken away from the relationship unless both agree that what replaces it is something better.

7. They agree that if the upset can't be resolved by working cooperatively with each other, they will seek outside help through therapy or some other available means.

Dealing with Blame and Guilt

Client Statements: "He/she is the cause of my problems."
"There must be something wrong with me that he/she treats me so badly."

Problem: People tend to blame their current relationship partner for things their parents did to them during childhood that they didn't like. Conversely, they also feel guilty because they believe they must have done something wrong. Many people believe they caused their parents much grief and they deserved the verbal and sometimes physical abuse they received. Some people feel guilty because of the pain they caused their mother during birth. Unless people somehow resolve these issues with their parents and with themselves, they will remain stuck in self-defeating patterns and literally never grow up.

Operating Principles

1. First I merely listen to understand what these clients may be feeling and how they are expressing themselves. I can usually tell fairly soon whether the client's energy is mostly in blaming others or blaming self.
2. I help clients see that the sources of their present conflicts are rooted in the past and, as such, have little to do with their present situation.
3. Then I start a reeducative process designed to help the client let go of negative beliefs and feelings and learn how to grow up emotionally. This process includes:
   a. surfacing and expressing all feelings toward the parents that have been left unexpressed since childhood.
   b. experiencing the reality that emotionally parents were once children themselves and were programmed to behave the way they did toward their children.
   c. forgiving or giving back to the parents that which was theirs in the first place and beginning to see them as they really are.
   d. completing the same process with oneself.
4. The next phase involves helping the client get used to life the way it really is and not the way he or she thought it was or should be.

5. Finally, I spend time helping the client experience loving himself or herself and others in an ever expanding and deepening context.

Therapeutic Tools

The primary issue in dealing with this pattern is to clear karmatic links that often go back endlessly in the client's family. By helping clients break with the negative patterns they got from their parents, I can help them avoid perpetuating these patterns with their children. Once clients bring their true feelings to the surface, and express them, they can better understand what was really going on. I try to help them see that no one taught their parents how to love and, therefore, they could not be expected to teach their children how to do something they could not do themselves.

Some of these negative love patterns can surely be traced back to the first man and woman. These patterns are the most common and most contagious "dis-eases" in the history of the world. People have gotten off course a long time ago and have stayed off course since then. Now, by a shift in perception and a willingness to view themselves differently, people have available the necessary tools to get them back on course.

In the early stages of helping clients identify childhood sources for their current problems, I often rely on a variety of written activities. Later, I may use structured experiences, gestalt techniques, and neurolinguistic programming techniques. Finally, I use breathing and visualizations to help clients experience loving themselves and others.

Therapeutic Tool #1: Facilitating Blame.[4] I learned of this tool somewhat accidentally. Some years ago a former client of mine called and said that her husband of twenty-five years had left her and that she wanted to get some supportive therapy. I suggested that she join an ongoing therapy group I was running. She agreed

---

4. From Barry Weinhold and Lynn Elliott, *Transpersonal Communication* (Englewood Cliffs, NJ: Prentice-Hall, 1979).

and, although she found some support from the group, she seemed really stuck, unable to mobilize any resources for herself outside the therapy situation. Yet, in the group she was trying to be a model client, always owning her part in the problem and being objective about her husband. Finally I asked her to contract with the group to blame her husband for everything. The only limit we had was that if we were tired of hearing her complaints, we could ask her to stop. She did this faithfully each week until she had expressed every blaming thought and feeling she had ever had, and then she was ready to move on and put her life together again. This took about a month and may have saved years of therapeutic "stuckness."

Often I use the same approach with couples who are seemingly caught in a mutual pattern of blame. First I ask the two to take turns blaming everything that has happened in a disputed incident on the other person. Then I ask them to blame everything that has happened on themselves. Finally I ask them to go over the incident a third time, taking account of their responsibility (ability to respond) and determining how much of that responsibility they actually used in the situation. Generally, this part of the process enables couples to see clearly what they did and what they could have done. This awareness becomes a basis for handling future disagreements.

Therapeutic Tool #2: The Resentment Release. Foregiveness literally means "to give back," or to let go of longstanding resentment. The following case example illustrates the use of breathing techniques to facilitate the process of forgiveness.

Mrs. Long, who was 64 at the time, had been suffering from crippling arthritis of the spine and had been on heavy pain medication for some time. She had difficulty walking and spent more and more time in a wheelchair. The doctors, after examining her thoroughly, told her they could do nothing further for her and that she likely would be confined to a wheelchair for the rest of her life. She was unwilling to accept this bleak prognosis and came to see if I could help her.

While taking a short history, which she gave me in a rather whining, pathetic voice, she related troubles with her daughter, who hadn't spoken to her for twenty-some years, and stated how resentful Mrs. Long was that her own daughter would treat her so badly. She did not connect this with her present condition, but I did immediately. From my study of mind-body connections, I knew that the mental causation of arthritis was a lack of forgiveness and longstanding resentment.

I told her I believed the arthritis had resulted from her lack of forgiveness of her daughter and asked her if she would be willing to focus on forgiving her daughter as I taught her a breathing process designed to promote the release of resentment from the body. She agreed to do what she could to learn the process. I taught her a connective breathing process and watched carefully as she lay on her back breathing. Things began to happen quickly. Her body began to shake, and she began to cry softly. I reassured her that she was experiencing the beginning of the release process, and I instructed her to continue breathing. As she did so, the shaking intensified, then finally subsided. Later she reported that during this process she had the sensation of a physical mass rising out of her spine and leaving her body. Her hands, which had been stiffened by arthritis, now were flexible. As she flexed her hands repeatedly, she exclaimed with tears of joy running down her cheeks, "It's gone! I feel like a new person. I can't believe it. It's a miracle."

Following the one session, she continued to improve while practicing her breathing an hour every day. She reported no longer feeling resentful toward her daughter and having forgiven her completely. In my follow-up contacts with Mrs. Long after that one session almost three years ago, she reports that she has not taken a single pain pill since that session and still has no pain or discomfort. Her overall attitude is positive. Her remarkable recovery has been an inspiration to her friends and relatives, and she is often asked to speak to church groups, as well as to teach them the release breathing that I showed her.

This case illustrated for me the potency of using a mind-body approach to forgiveness. The timing of my intervention, plus Mrs.

Long's willingness to trust me and her belief that this process could help, certainly were contributing factors in the success of this case. I have not achieved the same quick, dramatic results with others, but I have found that this approach does produce remarkable results over time for most clients.

9

Personality Issues In Psychological and Spiritual Growth

Gay Hendricks

Both in my own life and in my work as a therapist, I have often puzzled over several related paradoxes in the realm of psychological and spiritual growth. Most seekers want to transcend the limitations of their personalities so that they can experience their essence directly and permanently. Why, then, do we often encounter the most difficult obstacles in the physical world immediately after a breakthrough to a new awareness on the spiritual or psychological level? Why do people in intimate relationships create major upsets following a period of intense closeness? Why does a time of deep meditation often bring to the surface the most crystallized elements of our personality?

Over the last few years I have developed some ideas of about what accounts for these seeming incongruities. At the same time, I have been working toward the development of processes that allow us to deal effectively with issues of personality that seem to emerge strongly in people who are working on their spiritual or psychological liberation.

WHAT IS MEANT BY "PERSONALITY ISSUES?"

Anything that emerges more than once from the ground of one's being can be considered a personality issue. Examples of personality are:

- ritualized patterns of interaction (e.g., arguments with similar styles and themes, "games" in the sense that Eric Berne used the term, the tendency to withdraw and sulk when hurt).
- ritualized styles of thinking (e.g., beliefs such as "I'm unlovable," worry, the tendency to make oneself right or wrong).
- feelings that recycle (e.g., always being scared in the presence of authority figures, feeling lonely in a crowd, having anger toward men or women regardless of their role).
- limiting habits and patterns in the body (e.g., psychosomatic disorders, excess tension, imbalanced carriage).

When using the term *personality*, I refer to the *content* of consciousness as contrasted with consciousness itself, the *context*.

WHY WOULD PERSONALITY EMERGE STRONGLY WHILE PURSUING PSYCHOLOGICAL OR SPIRITUAL LIBERATION?

A common trap that occasionally snares seekers is the attitude that something is wrong with personality. Frequently, in beginning a quest for liberation, one carries into the initial stages of it the styles of thinking that are common to the ordinary, shackled mind. A typical style of thinking is that one thing is better than another — e.g., enlightenment is better than being stuck, or one path is better than another path. As the quest progresses, one may dissolve comparative styles of thinking, but until then, such patterns are characteristic of its early stages. In fact, holding the view that personality is not as good as, say, essence, is one of the bolts that holds the personality firmly in place.

By pushing hard in one direction, one is likely to create a strong vector in the opposite direction. Pushing hard to grow on the spiritual and psychological levels often has the effect of bringing up problems in other areas, such as the physical and the relationship levels. Setting high spiritual goals tends to invite problems in the physical world — not as a test, but as an opportunity to integrate what one has learned on the spiritual level with the level of everyday reality. If a breakthrough in meditation is followed by a flat tire, fixing a flat can be a perfect place to practice one's newfound awareness.

If viewing personality issues negatively both perpetuates them and is inaccurate, what, then, is a clearer picture of their role in spiritual and psychological growth? Perhaps the most evolved view is to regard personality and essence as one and the same: They are equal expressions of an overall creative oneness. The emergence of personality can then be seen as no better or no worse than anything else. On the way to developing the maximally spacious point of view, it may be useful to regard the emergence of personality in a positive light, in part as an antidote to the long-held bleak view of one's darker side.

Personality issues may be viewed in several positive ways. One way is to see them as healthy signs of growth. When exploring a dusty room in the dark, one does not see all the cleaning that is needed. By lighting a candle, though, the extent of the problem immediately becomes clearer. At this point, one can choose to view the work to be done in a positive or a negative way.

Meditation and other growth tools are like lights in that they increase our ability to see. If what we see is not pleasant, this surely cannot be meditation's fault.

I am now approaching my tenth year of regular meditation, approximately one-and-a-half hours each day. The first year was not much fun, as I looked into some very dusty and cluttered corners of my mind. But after that, I seemed to become more comfortable with truth than with illusion. As bad as it was, I would rather see it than not see it. Then it all changed, and I began to feel good about it. At this point the noise and clutter dropped to relatively low levels and have continued to decrease over the years.

The need for grounding while pursuing a spiritual path cannot be minimized. By grounding I mean those processes by which we stabilize and anchor in everyday life those things we have learned through spiritual growth. If personality issues emerge strongly after a leap to a new level of spiritual awareness, one has the opportunity to deal with those very issues to which the new awareness needs to be most urgently applied in daily living, where we spend most of our time.

PRIOR TECHNOLOGIES

Several technologies for dealing with personality issues have been developed in times past. None of these seems suited to the large numbers of people engaging in psychological and spiritual practices in contemporary society. One prior technology involved withdrawal from the world into a role in which the rules and rituals for daily life were rigidly prescribed. I am referring here to the monastic disciplines, developed several thousand years ago in the East and over the past thousand years in the West. By withdrawing from the world, monks are able to deal with personality by avoiding close relationships, seeking solitude, and following rules laid down by the authorities of their order.

The central concept of another technology has been to deny, ignore, or minimize the manifestation of personality. This position presumes that personality issues are of a lower order of things than the "real" work and are to be given a status equivalent to, say, a bowel movement — necessary, perhaps, but to be dispatched quickly with as little ado as possible.

A NEW TECHNOLOGY

We need to develop a new way to handle personality that is based on what we have learned in psychology over the past generation or two. One of the major insights of our time, perhaps of all time, is that *what we resist runs us,* that the most efficient way to be rid of something is not to ignore or deny it, but to integrate it into the totality of ourselves. Any technology not based on this principle is out of date.

What does such a process, based on a principle of integration, look like? It would be a process in which we could let personality manifest itself and be integrated so as to enhance our ability to experience love and truth. It would allow personality to slip through us effortlessly and be dealt with by experiencing it, expressing it clearly, and learning to love it. Specifically, the process involves some or all of the following elements.

1. *Witnessing or noticing the manifestation of one's personality in the form of thoughts, behavior, feelings, or body sensations.* The more practice one has in the process, the faster one seems able to catch the personality in early phases of manifestation. For example, in the early stage of noticing the personality, a man may catch it only after he has started an agrument with his wife by saying, "You're flirting too much with Sam." With more practice he may catch such a manifestation earlier, when it is a feeling in his body and some thoughts in his mind: "Honey, I feel afraid when you talk to Sam like you did last night at the party." In the latter observation he captured his own inner experience without projecting it onto his wife in the form of criticism or value judgment.

2. *Taking full responsibility for the element of personality that is manifesting.* Frequently we do not notice the personality until it has emerged from ourselves and been projected on others or the environment. In mastering the personality, it is vital that we notice it and assume full responsibility for it.

3. *Experiencing this element of personality directly, as opposed to thinking about it, analyzing it, dramatizing it, or efforting to get rid of it.* One of the most amazing things I have learned in doing therapy over the years is that *insight follows experience.* Until a person is willing to experience fear of something, for example, attempts to understand it will be largely empty intellectual exercises. After experiencing the fear, insights seem to flow organically and effortlessly.

4. *Communicating about experiences clearly from a position of responsibility.* If one is in an appropriate position to do it, verbal communication is an important way to bring about personality integration. Communicating clearly about one's experience seems to promote growth by making space for the next deepest level of truth to emerge.

5. *Loving it.* The quickest way I have found of integrating an element of the personality is to love it. Of course, one has to experience *not loving it* before the experience of loving it can happen. I have seen difficult elements of the personality, from obesity to depression to *anorexia nervosa*, cleared up by persons coming to love those parts of themselves.

To illustrate, I will use examples drawn from three realms: meditation, therapy, and intimate relationships.

Meditation

I sit down to meditate. I begin to let a mantra[1] resonate in my mind. Over the next half hour my mind goes back and forth between thoughts and the mantra. As meditation deepens, there is less thought. The mantra repeats itself at subtler and subtler levels until what remains is quiet space. Occasionally thoughts will float through, and I see them pass as though I am watching the clouds pass through the sky.

The attitude that seems to make this process possible is not minding thoughts. My meditation teacher taught me that thoughts are a positive sign that meditation is working. Stress is releasing from the body and mind, and thoughts are an indication of a deeper positive process. Thus, thoughts are not to be dramatized, fretted over, or taken seriously in any sense. They just *are*. When I found myself lost in thought I was to gently bring myself back to the mantra.

By studying the process of meditation, I have learned important lessons about all of life. I have learned that personality issues can manifest in the form of all sorts of thoughts and feelings, and I can simply let this happen without attaching unnecessary energy

---

1. The mantra is a mellifluous syllable of Sanskrit derivation.

to the process. Also, I have learned how to let go, to get off a train of thought, seductive as it might be, and relax into just *being* again. After experiencing this process thousands of times in meditation, I have come to regard the process of letting go as one of the fundamental arts of life.

Therapy

One of the major functions of therapy is in helping clients learn effective processes of relating to their personalities. I know a man who was working deeply on himself to clear up a decade-long siege of conflict between him and his former wife. Much effort had gone into learning the process I am describing here. One day the man was resting at home when he found himself thinking about, in his words, "what a jerk my ex-wife is." Instead of indulging this projection of his mind, he was able to catch his personality right in the process of manifesting and channel the energy into a more effective strategy. He took responsibility for the anger he felt and allowed himself to experience it in his body. Immediately a wave of compassion swept over him.

He next took responsibility for the part of himself that is a "jerk." He found a place in his body that represented the part of himself that felt that way. He opened up to it and tuned into the feeling that seemed to be stored in that area. He experienced several gusts of fear and sadness. Then, spontaneously, he experienced love for both himself and his ex-wife. It was one of the first times in the history of their conflict that he recalls feeling a clear, positive regard toward her.

One might note several particulars of this process. When the personality began to emerge, in the form of the "she's a jerk" thought, he did not take it seriously and continue to run this train of thought. He took it as something of his own manufacture and turned it into an opportunity to get high from it rather than letting his mind become a go-cart track of recycling negative thoughts. By stepping in with a new process, he created a transformation.

Intimate Relationships

Intimate relationships are a particularly rigorous proving ground for any process because the very nature of such relationships is to give us our strongest experience of love — thus creating space for our strongest resistance to love to emerge. Often when we think a relationship is not working, what is actually happening is that it has worked so well that it has created space for more personality to emerge than can be smoothly integrated. This is why so many marital splits occur after a period of intense closeness.

For example, a crisis emerged with a couple I know when the husband had an extramarital affair. The wife, having done a great deal of work on herself in mastering the process with which we are concerned here, chose to not treat the situation as a transgression but as an opportunity for deeper mastery. Rather than trying to manipulate the environment to get it to quit making her feel badly, which she could have done by demanding that her husband stop the affair, she took responsibility for the situation and assumed that she was creating it in part because she needed to learn something.

As she started dipping deeply into her own experience, she found that beneath a surface layer of hurt and anger toward her husband, she was experiencing a deep fear of being abandoned. When she looked into this feeling, she realized that it had been around since she was a child. After realizing this, she had a conversation with her husband in which she thanked him for bringing this fear to her attention. She told him that she was willing to deal with the issue herself, without further assistance from him, and so he could have the affair or not, but entirely for his own purposes. Interestingly enough, he soon ended the other relationship, and to my current knowledge they are experiencing growth and continued pleasure in their marriage.

The attitude that made this transformation possible was the wife's willingness to treat what was manifesting, even though she was seemingly not the active participant, as something for which she, too, was responsible.

Many relationships bog down in a tedious attempt by one or the other member to prove that what is happening ought not to be happening. If we regard what is happening as what ought to be happening, we are in a much stronger position to transform any situation.

A process based on integration of manifesting personality elements can allow for the natural process of living to be regarded as part of one's path. In this way, we do not partition off one part of life from another, but regard all as part of the whole.

10

Meditation
in the Art of Therapy

Gay Hendricks

Meditation is an important tool in the practice of therapy. What meditation is, why it works, and how it can be useful in therapy are the major subjects of discussion in this chapter.

WHAT IS MEDITATION?

Meditation refers to an array of techniques, predominantly mental, designed to help practitioners dissolve mental, physical, and emotional blocks to unity within themselves, with others, and with the universe. The techniques often consist of mental practices that tend to obstruct, turn down the volume on, or render transparent the workings of the conscious mind, in order to facilitate the growth of other faculties such as intuition, as well as transpersonal values and experiences such as being, bliss, oneness, compassion, and self-realization.

I first meditated in 1969. In my first meditation I had such a powerful experience that I did not do it again until 1973. Using a meditation practice that I got from a yoga book, I sat down and began mentally repeating the mantra, *OM.* Within seconds my mind, usually teeming with thoughts, fell utterly silent, as if I were seeing myself clearly for the first time without the intervening fog of thoughts. I felt as if I had removed for a moment a raccoon coat I had been wearing all my life.

Until that moment, everything I had experienced had been filtered through my thoughts. For the moment, the filter was removed and I saw myself, and the world, as I was. Scared by this insight, I stopped meditating immediately. Looking back on the incident, I do not feel as if I were ready to see things the way they actually are.

In 1973 I was properly instructed by a qualified teacher in how to meditate. Since then I have meditated twice daily for about twenty minutes each session until 1979, when I increased the time to about forty-five minutes per session. The changes meditation has brought about in my life and work have been profound. I would like to describe some of them.

First, how does meditation feel? I begin by sitting in a quiet place, either in a chair or on a cushion on the floor. I use a mantra meditation, so after a minute or so of sitting quietly with my eyes closed, I begin to gently think the mantra. Thoughts come and go. When I find myself lost in thought, I gently return to the mantra. As the meditation deepens, I usually encounter periods of no thought, when all is quiet save the rhythm of the mantra. Then, often, the mantra fades away, leaving behind a quiet, light space of silence. During meditation the typical experience is one of silence. Occasionally, waves of bliss pass through my body and mind, and sometimes solutions to problems pop into my mind. The experience during meditation is generally unspectacular. The results of meditation in my life *are* spectacular.

First, I feel vastly more relaxed in all areas of my life since I began meditating. Ten years ago one of my friends described me as "a very uptight guy." I chain-smoked two to three packs of cigarettes a day, bit my nails to the quick, and was fifty pounds overweight. I also had an incipient case of ulcers. All those problems have cleared up during these years of regular meditation.

A direct benefit of meditation in my counseling work has been that I can more easily pay attention, with a quiet mind, to my own feelings. By learning to listen to my own inner experience, I have also learned to listen to deeper levels of what my clients are saying.

I have also noticed a marked upsurge in intuition and telepathic communication, particularly in the last few years. I believe that these processes occur naturally in us all but that other thought processes are so noisy that they obscure the subtler levels of thought. Of course, the challenge in identifying intuition and psychic processes is learning how to discriminate them from thoughts generated by fear. For example, on your way to the airport you may have a thought of the airplane crashing. Most often, thoughts such as this are just surface noise from underlying fear.

In my experience, I have found two ways to discriminate intuitions from ordinary thought. An example will illustrate. As I was meditating one morning, a picture of a person I was to see later in the day appeared in my mind. I had not seen him in fifteen years. In my mind I heard him say, "My mother died of cancer about a year ago." The thought had a certain quality to it that somehow made it different from other thoughts. Later, when I saw my client I asked him how his family was. Fine, he said, except that, "My mother died of cancer about a year ago."

One way, then, I have learned to tell intuition from ordinary thinking is to notice different qualities that intuitive thoughts have. A second way is to notice whether any fear is present in you at the time of the thought. This observation may help you in determining whether the thought is fear-based. Above all, of course, is the need to check out empirically whether or not the thought has any relation to reality.

SOME VARIETIES OF MEDITATION

We have information, either through writings or through the transmission of students who have studied under qualified teachers, on a substantial number of meditation techniques. Just as many, if not more, techniques probably exist on which we have no information, largely since they are intended for use only within a certain cultural context or because they are intended to be used with the time, place, and nature of the student in mind. An extended listing of meditation practices is beyond the scope of this chapter, but I would like to describe a few techniques in sufficient detail to acquaint clinicians with the use of meditation in therapy. Readers who wish to explore classifications of techniques more thoroughly should see some of the excellent books on this subject.[1]

The three forms of meditation that I describe here are the ones with which I have most experience in therapy. They are Vipassana meditation from the Theravadan Buddhist tradition, bare attention, and Transcendental Meditation.

Vipassana (Insight) Meditation

The Vipassana meditation, from the Theravadan (Southern) Buddhist tradition, is practiced primarily in Burma, Sri Lanka, Thailand, and parts of India. In recent years Vipassana meditation has expanded in Europe, the United Kingdom, and the United States.

Joseph Goldstein, a Westerner who has studied in the East for many years, began offering workshops and retreats some years ago in which he taught the fundamentals of the Vipassana meditation. His book, *The Experience of Insight*, contains meditation instructions woven among insights, stories, and observations about the nature of the mind and spiritual unfoldment.[2] Here are several quotes from that book:

> It is important to make thoughts the object of mindfulness. If we remain unaware of thoughts as they arise, it is difficult to develop insight

---

1. Some of the most informative books available on meditation are Robert Ornstein's *The Psychology of Consciousness* (New York: Penguin, 1975); Claudio Naranjo and Robert Ornstein's *On The Psychology Of Meditation* (New York: Viking Press, 1971); and John White's *What Is Meditation?* (New York: Anchor Books, 1972).
2. Joseph Goldstein, *The Experience of Insight* (Santa Cruz, CA: Unity Press, 1976).

into their impersonal nature and into our own deep-rooted and subtle identification with the thought process.

> It is helpful to make a mental note of "thinking, thinking" every time a thought arises. . . . The thought is the thinker. There is no one behind it. The thought is thinking itself. It comes uninvited. . . . Some people may find it helpful to label the thinking process in a more precise way, to note different kinds of thoughts, whether "planning" or "imagining" or "remembering."

> Awareness of the breath can be practiced in one or two ways. When you breathe in, the abdomen naturally rises or extends and when you breathe out, it falls. Keep your attention on the movement of the abdomen, not imagining, not visualizing anything, just experiencing the sensation of the movement. . . .

> The alternative is to be aware of the breath as it goes in and out of the nostrils, keeping the attention around the tip of the nose or the upper lip. . .

> Simply be aware of the in and out breath as it passes the nostrils. It is helpful in the beginning of the practice to make mental notes either of "rising, falling" or "in, out." This aids in keeping the mind on the object.

The essence of the Vipassana practice, as illustrated in the preceding quotes, is the observation and mental labeling of all the events that enter the practitioner's field of consciousness. The observation and labeling eventually give way to a state of bare attention, a pure awareness of everything that is not contaminated with even the most innocent of concepts (such as labeling). The labeling, then, is seen as a helpful process designed to point the practitioner toward the purer process of bare attention.

Bare Attention

Bare attention refers to a quality of mind that is nonevaluative, noncomparative — simple observation of things as they are. This quality of mind, in both client and therapist, can be highly useful in therapy. Many teachers have spoken of the value of bare attention. Again, to quote from Joseph Goldstein:

> This quality of bare attention is well expressed by a famous Japanese haiku:
>
> > The old pond.
> > A frog jumps in.
> > Plop!

> No dramatic description of the sunset and the peaceful evening sky over the pond and how beautiful it was. Just a crystal clear perception of what it was that happened. . . . Bare attention; learning to see and observe, with simplicity and directness. Nothing extraneous. It is a powerfully penetrating state of mind. The Buddhist Walpola Rahula described a similar process.

> "Another very important, practical and useful form of meditation (mental development) is to be aware and mindful of whatever you do, physically or verbally, during the daily routine of work in your life, private, public or professional. Whether you walk, stand, sit, lie down or sleep, whether you stretch or bend your limbs, whether you look around, whether you put on your clothes, whether you talk or keep silent, whether you eat or drink — even whether you answer the calls of nature — in these and other activities you should be fully aware of the act performed at the moment.

Krishnamurti, the Indian spiritual teacher who has been talking and writing on meditation and related subjects for the past sixty years, described the meditative state of mind as one of "choiceless awareness." By this phrase, he seems to mean a constant state of nonevaluative attentiveness to all of life processes. In the same vein, a Zen master was once asked to divulge the key to enlightenment. "Attention" was his answer. When asked to say more about this cryptic reply, he said, "Attention, attention, attention." Yes, but what does attention mean, asked the bewildered disciple. "Attention," replied the master, "means attention."

In the context of therapy, bare attention can be applied during the therapy session as a formal technique, or informally in the client's daily life. Bare attention may be applied to behavior, thoughts, feelings, sensation, intentions, perceptions, beliefs, opinions, or any other experience. Bare attention is simply the practice of using the natural observational powers of the mind.

Transcendental Meditation

Transcendental meditation, commonly known as TM, is a technique, from the Indian tradition, going back several thousand years. It was brought to the West by Maharishi Mahesh Yogi, who credits his teacher and long succession of spiritual masters with preserving the technique in a pure form for dozens of generations. TM is probably the most widely practiced meditation technique in the West and has been the subject of several books.

After studying the effects of TM through observing its effects on clients, personally experiencing it, and reading the research literature that has grown up around it, I began several years ago to recommend its practice to clients who seemed interested in it.

TM is a simple technique that requires no special postures, diets, clothing, or life style. The technique is performed twice daily, usually before breakfast and dinner, for twenty minutes each time. After initial instruction, which takes place over four days, participation in activities sponsored by the local TM center is purely voluntary. One such activity, which in my opinion is easily worth the instruction fee, is called "checking." This consists of a procedure to verify the correct practice of TM and allows the practitioner to get answers to questions or advice for dealing with any difficulties that emerge from practice of the technique.

Mechanics of this technique, which must be learned from a teacher, include repetition of a mellifluous syllable(s) in a relaxed, attentive manner, a few technical instructions on how the mantra is to be used, but little else. The practitioner does not have to adopt any particular attitudes or beliefs or do anything special aside from the twice-daily period of meditation.

WAYS OF USING MEDITATION IN THERAPY

My method of using the types of meditation just discussed varies from client to client, but it usually consists of one of three procedures. I teach many clients the Vipassana technique and bare attention over several sessions as part of the counseling. Frequently my procedure is to leave ten to fifteen minutes open at the end of several sessions to teach the basics of the techniques.

Another procedure, which I incorporated more recently, is to put the instructions for the techniques on cassette tape recordings so that the client can listen to an instruction and practice a phase of the technique either before or after the therapy session. For the Vipassana technique and bare attention, the instructions are recorded on eight to ten separate cassettes, to be listened to on as many separate occasions. For example, the client may learn to apply bare attention to thoughts on one occasion, then return the following week to learn and practice the observation of sensations. With TM, clients make their own arrangements to learn the technique.

After initial instructions, clients practice the techniques in a variety of ways. In my work, clients are asked to practice at home once or twice daily for ten or fifteen minutes, or to follow the instructions for TM, which specify that the practice should be done twice daily for twenty minutes. Sometimes I ask clients to meditate with me for a while, particularly at the beginning and end of sessions.

EFFECTS OF MEDITATION

Various explanations for the effects of meditation have been set forth. The discussion begins with those that are most consonant with prevailing scientific views, then ventures afield into explanations that rest on spiritual or metaphysical underpinnings.

Meditation as a Relaxant

The current upsurge of interest in meditation can be traced to publication of a condensed version of R. K. Wallace's doctoral dissertation in *Scientific American*, February 1972, which presented data that attributed changes in a number of dependent measures to Transcendental Meditation. The variables studied were oxygen consumption and blood lactate concentrate, which are related to states of deep relaxation. Wallace and his co-author, Herbert Benson, called the meditative state "wakeful, hypometabolic," since meditation seemed to bring about a condition of the organism that was as relaxed as, and sometimes more relaxed than, sleep but that let the meditator remain in a wakeful state. Following the pioneering work by Wallace and Benson, many other studies confirmed and extended these initial findings.

Meditation might be expected to bring about a decrease in physiological arousal for several reasons. One theory, proposed by Dr. Bernard Glueck of the Institute of Living in Hartford, Connecticut, is that the mentally-repeated sound (mantra) used in some forms of meditation may set up resonant derivatives that enter the limbic system of the brain at the right frequency to dampen limbic hyperarousal. In addition, one body in the limbic system, the hypothalamus, is known to regulate activities of the hormone system and the autonomic nervous system.

In a recent book on Transcendental Meditation, the authors suggested that meditation may bring about a state of quiescence in the hypothalamus, thus fostering a more efficient tone of the parasympathetic branch of the autonomic nervous system.[3] Further, they pointed out that quiescence of the hormonal system could be expected to bring about lessened alarm reactions, thus increasing the meditator's ability to tolerate stress. Finally, the authors ventured farther afield to suggest that meditation may bring about a hypersynchrony of brain waves between the cortex and the lower, visceral brain centers such as the limbic and the brain stem, thereby healing the age-old split between emotion and reason.

This viewpoint is close to my own theory of meditation's effects. In my view, we experience a conflict between essence —that which we truly are — and the functioning of the ego, including emotion and reason. Essence is that part of us that is free from conditioning, and ego is that part of us that has been adopted for survival and safety reasons. The conflict between ego and essence may keep us in a state of autonomic hyperarousal.

Since many forms of meditation offer the opportunity to alternate between being aware of essence and being lost in ego, the practice may bring the conflict to the level of awareness, thus enabling the meditator to transcend the conflict. In addition, experiencing essence, which is usually overshadowed by ego, may give the individual a basic sense of self that can heal the split, enabling the meditator to lessen and dissolve the tension that theretofore had accompanied the split.

Meditation as Discrimination Training

Most forms of meditation involve an alternation between a state of attentiveness and being identified with the contents of consciousness. Anyone who has meditated for even fifteen minutes recognizes the constant alternation between the object of meditation (e.g., breath, or a mantra) and being "lost in thought."

Most of the esoteric disciplines consider thought to be one of the major barriers to the harmonious and holistic development of

---

3. H. Bloomfield, M. Cain, R. Joffe, and R. Kory, *TM: Overcoming Stress and Discovering Inner Energy* (New York: Delacorte Press, 1975).

consciousness. These disciplines teach that attachment to and identification with thought prevents us from attaining an ego-free state of nonattachment. The esoteric disciplines have developed many meditative practices designed to correct this situation by detaching the practitioner from thought. Patanjali, for example, wrote 1,500 years ago that "yoga is the control of thought waves in the mind." Don Juan, the Yacqui Indian sorcerer, instructed Carlos to "turn off the internal dialogue," and the Zen discipline features not only meditative practices but also koans, or questions with no logical solution, to disrupt the flow of ordinary thought.

The mechanics of most meditation techniques involve a process of moving back and forth between being "lost in thought" and a state of attentiveness. To illustrate, Transcendental Meditation makes use of a mentally-repeated Sanskrit word or phrase (a mantra). The key instruction in TM is to return to the mantra whenever the practitioner notices himself or herself thinking. Thus, the meditator is continually alternating between periods of thought and repetitions of the mantra. Diagrammed, a sequence of meditation might be experienced as follows:

Om
↓
Om
↓
Om
↓
Image of clock . . .
↓
"I wonder how long I've been meditating?"
↓
Om
↓
Om
↓
Om
↓
Sensation from leg going to sleep . . .
↓
Om
↓
etc.

Similarly, one of the instructions in the Zen discipline is to count breaths from one to ten, starting over when the meditator loses attention. The point is that both TM and Zen, along with other techniques, use a process of alternation between thought and attentiveness.

In physiological psychology and learning theory, the phrase *discrimination training* is used to describe the process by which an organism acquires the ability to differentiate between and among stimuli. In one hour's meditation, a practitioner may have hundreds of experiences of being identified with thought, then returning to a more attentive state. This process can be regarded as discrimination training, since the meditator is learning to discriminate thought from other stimuli.[4]

Being skilled at discriminating thought from other events puts the meditator in a particularly strong position of mental health. Thoughts are prominent components of most mental health problems such as depression, anxiety, and schizophrenia. In fact, one could argue that, since nearly everyone has a certain number of neurotic thoughts, mental health is dependent upon the ability to recognize that they are "just thoughts." The depressed person is so identified with thoughts (e.g., "I'm no good") that he or she takes them for fact, rather than realizing that they are just products of his mind. Clinically, I have found that clients who are given meditation experiences to learn to discriminate thought characteristically regard the outcome as a revelation. As one client said,

> I would carry on long conversations in my head. I would fantasize future possibilities and base my actions on them. After Dr. _____ trained me to see my thoughts, I felt a tremendous sense of liberation. My God, there was nothing to worry about — they were just thoughts.

Once this individual could observe her thoughts and was no longer identified with them, she was free to choose whether or not to base her behavior on them.

In addition, most persons agree that being in the "here and now" is a positive goal from both a psychological and a spiritual perspective. Since thought is what usually takes us out of the here

---

4. C. G. Hendricks, "Theoretical Note: Meditation as Discrimination Training," *Journal of Transpersonal Psychology*, 1975, 2, pp. 144-146.

and now, discrimination training through meditation is helpful by clarifying when we are thinking. This clarity increases the freedom of choice of whether to remain in the thinking state or to return attention to the here and now.

One of the major goals of meditation is to see things as they are. The discrimination training function of meditation makes the contents of consciousness more visible, allowing the meditator more choice as to whether or not to identify with them.

Meditation as Training in Becoming Disidentified With One's Point-of-View

Our point-of-view is a subtle perceptual state that literally means the point from which we view the world. It is a screen through which we see the world, a screen that can be dense or porous depending on our history of conditioning and our previous attempts to gain awareness. Do we see the world as a frightening place full of hostile people? A competitive place with not enough to go around? These are examples of points-of-view that I have seen clients recognize and give up during the course of therapy.

Point-of-view is difficult to dissolve because when we are seeing the world from a certain perspective, that is the way we think the world is. By penetrating to the subtler levels of conditioning, meditation affords an opportunity to observe our point-of-view. Once seen, it can be dropped.

The process of dissolving identification with the point(s)-of-view is basically the same one discussed earlier as discrimination training. By alternating back and forth between being stuck in the point-of-view and being in an attentive state free from the conditioned perceptions of the point-of-view, the meditator gains an ability to see how his or her point of view colors the world.

Meditation as De-automatization

Arthur Deikman, a San Francisco psychiatrist, has advanced the theory that meditation is a process of de-automatization. The concept is meaningful in terms of the approach to therapy described in this book.

Some mystical traditions regard humans as being unconscious or "asleep" while they are responding out of their conditioning. Gurdjieff, for example, based his work upon the idea that conscious effort must be exerted in order to stay awake and "remember oneself." He and others regarded the asleep state as not making full use of the human capability at this stage of evolution.

Deikman performed some experiments on meditation in which meditators contemplated a vase for several sessions. Afterward, some of the meditators responded that their perceptions of the vase had changed as a result of the meditation. To some it appeared fresher, as if they were continually picking up new aspects of it. Others reported that it became more vivid and meaningful. Based on these data, Deikman proposed that the process of meditation somehow revivified the perception that had become automatic. He suggested that the brain tunes out stimuli as it habitually responds to the world, thus restricting our awareness. Meditation breaks up the automatic responses, cutting through conditioned perception to uncover a fresher, more direct grasp of reality.

This view fits with the view of meditation held by some of the spiritual disciplines. In the Christian tradition, the Scriptures say that unless we see through the eyes of a child, we cannot enter the kingdom of heaven. This can be taken to mean that mystic perception is reserved for those who can cut through their layers of conditioning to see the world as freshly as a child. Similarly, many of the Zen teachings explore the theme of learning to see the world each moment as new and fresh. We have the story of the Zen master who is chased over the side of a cliff by a tiger. He grasps at the branch of a bush growing out of the side of the cliff. From beneath he hears the roar of another tiger. There he hangs, unable to go up or down. Suddenly he sees a juicy-looking berry growing from the bush. He plucks it and eats it with great enjoyment.

Physiological research on Zen meditators supports the idea of meditation as keeping the perceptions fresh. Several accomplished Zen meditators took part in a study that subjected them to a repeated "click" stimulus as they meditated. Normally, the EEG reflects a response to the stimulus for the first few times; then the response decreases as the person habituates to the stimulus. In the Zen meditators, however, habituation to the stimulus did not occur; the brains of the subjects continued to respond to each "click" as if it were the first.

Both physiological studies and the verbal reports of meditators seem, then, to suggest that meditation can alter our perceptual processes. The benefits in therapy are quite obvious. Most people who come to therapy are there, in part, because they have created unproductive cycles of thought, action, and feelings in their lives. The problem is one of automatic responses of a negative nature to situations in which those responses are inappropriate. Furthermore, many clients are in therapy because they cannot free themselves from events of the past; others are there because of existential crises concerning the meaning of life (i.e., the usual responses to life have lost meaning). In all cases I can think of, meditation, with its effects of dissolving automatic responses and freshening perceptions of the world, could be of value.

Meditation as Aid
to Holistic Brain Function _____

One of the most exciting areas of research in recent years has been the effort to understand differences between the left and right hemispheres of the brain. Although much more research is needed before definitive statements can be made, the predominant theories may be summarized as follows. The left hemisphere generally specializes in speech, logic, and linear thought, and the right hemisphere is the domain of intuition and a more holistic type of knowledge. Western culture generally has favored and thus reinforced the left hemisphere type of knowledge, to the neglect and possible underdevelopment of the right hemisphere type of knowledge. A whole person is one who has an integrated mind with logic and intuition working in harmony.

Meditation may have the effect of systematically blocking the linear function of the brain so that intuition is allowed to develop. An example is a form of meditation that uses a mantram. Repetition of the mantra, although it could be considered a left hemisphere operation, is not done for the purpose of logic or meaning. Rather, the mantra is repeated for its sonant or vibratory effects. Meditators are usually advised to disregard thought, to go back to repetition of the mantra, whenever they find themselves lost in thought.

During the course of our development, the brain's linear, logical function may be reinforced to the extent that it overshadows the intuitive function. Meditation, by putting the linear on "hold," may allow for growth of right hemisphere functioning and thus lead to a more integrated brain function.

Meditation as Quieter of Surface Noise

Most meditators would agree that the practice of meditation has the effect of quieting the surface "noise" of the mind. Early in the practice of meditation, considerable noise is present in the form of memories of the recent past (e.g., things that we have forgotten to do), plans for the future (e.g., what we will have for dinner that night), and the idle chatter of talk, to ourselves, to others, to no one in particular. As meditation continues, the noise dies down, giving us access to subtler levels of the mind.

One of the subtler levels that becomes accessible is feeling. With a quiet mind one is able to watch thought emerge from feeling. In addition, we can tune in more easily to the physical sensation associated with certain feeling states so that we can learn the differences between sadness, fear, anger, and other feelings. This is important because many people confuse feelings. They report anger, for example, when the deeper feeling beneath the anger is fear.

Another level of the mind that emerges as surface noise dissolves is desire or want. Most of us go about wanting things unconsciously, but the desire is buried beneath the surface so it cannot be seen. In meditation one can often spot desires so that they can be made public. While the desire is buried beneath the surface, it causes a tension, as if we are straining toward some unidentified object. As we make our desires conscious, we can decide whether they are worth putting energy toward. If not, they can be dropped.

Meditation as Facilitator of Self-Realization

A final view of the effects of meditation that we will consider here is meditation as a facilitator of self-realization. This traditional Hindu view holds that a permanent, unchanging part of us is identical to and part of the absolute. The realization (making real) of this self is the goal of spiritual growth.

The basic human problem is seen as a split between awareness of the relative and awareness of the absolute. The relative world is ever-changing. Problems arise and fall, desires ebb and flow, feelings come and go. Our thoughts are rapidly alternating among the positive-negative aspects of memory, fantasy, and chatter. Our problems stem from our identification with these unstable elements of ourselves. For instance, when we are in the grip of anger, we lose contact with the self, our common element with the absolute. One moment we are identified with the negative thought ("I'm a bad person"), and the next moment a positive thought crowds in ("No, that's wrong, I'm a beautiful child of the Universe"). We become so identified with the comings and goings of the relative world that we lose touch with the awareness of our own divinity within.

Meditation provides an opportunity to realize the self because it makes clearer the impermanent nature of the relative. In a half-hour's meditation we may experience the rising and falling of dozens, perhaps hundreds, of thoughts, feelings, opinions, points-of-view, physical sensations. When the elements of the relative are observed and experienced, they tend to dissolve, so that what is left is something that can be experienced on the self.[5]

The foregoing represents some varieties of meditation, what might account for its effects, and how it can be used in therapy. My personal recommendation is that we as therapists should meditate regularly, not only to experience the benefits cited earlier, but to lay an experiential groundwork for any practices we might recommend to clients. Also, just as the practice of hand-washing between patients has both symbolic and practical value to the healer who works with the body, meditation may offer to healers of the mind an opportunity to begin and end each day afresh, uncontaminated by either our self-generated psychological "germs" or the ones heaped upon us by our clients. In my opinion, the practice of therapy is the most demanding of vocations, and we need to take advantage of as many tools as possible to further our own evolution, as well as to protect ourselves from the stresses placed upon us by people with troubled lives. I have found meditation to be a valuable tool in our repertoire.

---

5. The self itself as permanent or as another impermanent feature constitutes a major difference between Hindu and Buddhist beliefs.

11

Transpersonal
Movement Therapy

Kathlyn T. Hendricks

Life is movement, from the motion of the tides to the life cycle of the human being. The way we move broadcasts our relationship to life. It is the bridge between what goes on inside and what we show the world. The way people move together reveals more about their relationships than anything they could possibly say in words.

Dance and movement rituals have formed the core of community life for thousands of years. Dance has demarcated the major life cycle experiences, the rites of passage, and acts of war. Healers were movers until the age of the mind-body dichotomy, and ancient communities recognized and honored the healing power of movement.

In the twentieth century, movement therapy has developed as a specialty in the field of psychology. Since its reemergence with the work of Marian Chace at St. Elizabeth's Hospital, Washington, DC, in 1942, dance/movement therapists have acknowledged the intrinsic life force in all people, the healing power of shared rhythms and expressed feelings. Dance/movement therapists work with all ages and populations — in psychiatric hospitals, prisons, geriatric residence programs, adolescent halfway house settings, special education programs, and private practice.

Movement is a universal language, and dance/movement therapists are trained to use that language to heal and enhance the quality of life.

The illustrations in this chapter are taken from my private practice as a movement therapist, using a transpersonal approach. Following a discussion of the basic principles of movement therapy, a section of movement experiments is included.

THE LIFE OF THE BODY

When a person moves, his or her total psychological process emerges. A trained therapist can see the life script, style of encountering the world, major problem areas, all in the way these phenomena are lived out in movement. Movement conveys truth. Since the body essentially fleshes out one's concepts and attitudes and has no mechanisms for lying, it reveals directly one's willingness to see and be the truth of moment-to-moment experience. Movement is the direct printout from the unconscious. When we move, we recreate the self. Movement is therefore the image of our continuity. What we tell ourselves about ourselves becomes embodied. One client, for example, was always told she had "mousy brown" hair. Eventually she came to see her hair that color instead of the blond it actually is, and to become her image of a mousy brown-haired woman.

When people move, their investment in life becomes visible, as does their relative degree of aliveness. The basic rhythm of life is expansion and contraction; all movement is rhythmic, its cadence arising out of the omnipresent pulsation of life energy. Transpersonal movement therapy allows the movement experience to represent the individual's personality and also to move through and beyond the individual's shell of defenses to a deep connectedness with the complete cycles of existence.

The process of the mover (*how* the mover moves) is the focus of movement therapy. The transformation point is upon encountering the unknown, the void before one risks the unexperienced, that juncture between the familiar pattern and the unimaginable. One client wrote a short poem about his experience of that edge:

To Move Without A Reason

Action that does no violence to the actor.
"Just move without any particular
reason."
She said.
"O.K." he said with the confidence
of one who found it easy to
follow directions.
. . . without a reason?
Frozen on hands and knees
Struck by a ray of paradox
in a place no thought can change.
Waiting.
The bubble of expectation pierced.
Waiting.

In movement, the therapist sees the client's willingness to choose and to change. As we grow up, most of us grow in. We limit ourselves to what works, what is functional, what takes less time. We gradually turn ourselves into shells where the inner life becomes dissociated from expression, conflicts with expression, or is denied entirely. For example, one client, while lying on the floor in an early therapy session, was responding to the suggestion to stretch and release. She raised her straight arms above her head slightly, then craned them back to her side, extended her arms directly sideward like one of those wooden Christmas dolls on a string, stretched her toes down momentarily, and stopped. That was the extent of her inner sense of "stretching and releasing — no three-dimensional movement, no whole-body stretch, no real surrender into contact with the floor.

The body is not just a vehicle to carry the head around. The collective late-twentieth-century human body contains large areas that are internally invisible, not felt, sensed, or imagined. This body literally feels less, interacts less with the environment, takes up as little space as possible, and moves only when the task at hand requires it. Expression and creativity have become obsolete or imbued with vaguely sinister overtones. Bertherat, a physical therapist and author, has outlined the problem clearly.

> At a very early age we acquire a minimal repertory of movement that we never think about any more. All our lives we repeat these few movements without questioning them, and without understanding that they represent only a very small sampling of our possibilities. The majority of us make use of a few variations of only about a hundred of the more than two thousand movements that the human being is capable of. But we'd never take seriously someone who suggested that we're physically deficient.[1]

A young, very troubled woman, discovered while lying down that she could suspend her leg in the air for nearly twenty minutes (try it!) before she could sense where her thigh was, what muscles were holding her leg in the air, and what could release that holding.

The reasons for this movement atrophy are manifold but are primarily generated in the conflicts created by trying to become what we are told we are as children: "You'd be so pretty if you'd . . ."; "You're not really hurt"; "Don't be too smart" (. . . pretty, successful); "Be still; don't be so loud"; and so on. The major signal that internalized conflicts are present is the word "tension."

Tension is the expression of separation from life, from the ground of being. Tension is the label for the process of rigidifying, withdrawing, withholding from life. Our bodies reflect that illusion of separateness: the stiff necks and knotted shoulders, immobile diaphragms and shallow breathing, the face-front march through life with no knowledge of the back, the shadow.

One can manipulate and squeeze and exercise the tension away, but whatever supports tension will recreate it until its deeper meaning is felt, understood, and expressed. Tension, resistance, and stuckness are the same — all signals of the need to experience more deeply.

---

1. T. Bertherat and C. Bernstein, *The Body Has Its Reasons* (New York: Pantheon, 1977), p. 38.

Tension in all its manifestations emerges throughout the therapy process, and in fact may be the significant presenting problem. The client's assumptions about tension should be addressed before inner sensing can even be approached. I frequently hear people say, "Oh, that's just a tense place," "I'm just tense today," or, most often, "I'd sure like to get rid of this tension," as if tension were an "it," outside experiential, body awareness, somehow correctable by the remedies we use for other disorders (e.g., take a pill for a headache). As one man, totally dominated by keeping an eye on things and keeping up with things, and with frequent headaches, said to me, "If I calmed down, I'd be boring."

People live their tensions and become their conflicts. Polarization, the pervasive either-or, supports much of the unhappiness and life-emptiness that I see in clients. The dichotomies of win-lose, love-hate, up-down, controlling-collapsing, and so forth, fight for dominance within the person, eventually immobilizing not only the structure but the life force as well.

PURPOSES OF TRANSPERSONAL MOVEMENT THERAPY

The major purposes of transpersonal movement therapy, as briefly discussed below, are to expand beyond conditioning, recover the self, create authentic movement, and achieve transcendence through movement.

Expanding Beyond Conditioning

Why focus on movement as a process in therapy? Does it have some intrinsic validity, or is it a therapeutic luxury? Many movement experiences have taught me crucial lessons about my own life process and have served my evolution as a therapist. Perhaps my deepest ongoing exploration has been to complete my relationship to fear, especially the fear of expressing myself. A recent movement experience illustrates this cycle of encountering tension, allowing sensation, acknowledging feelings, and moving through to a new experience of self.

At a free-form dance with African drummers one evening, I allowed myself to go into free fall, to really explore that sensation in movement. Letting go into gravity was the culmination of my experiences in relation to fear. An equivalent to my sensations that evening would be skydiving. I discovered that when I became totally soft against gravity instead of *holding* myself to keep from falling, holding myself in any particular attitude about the way I should be, or in any kind of a position, no matter how pretty or daring, I became a kind of movement gyroscope. For about three hours I moved continually, letting go of the position in space or the pattern of moving over and over. As a result, I felt balanced in any position at all. I didn't fall, no matter what I did or how much I turned and leaped. I didn't find any limits in my ability to be grounded and to be simultaneously in motion. It felt as if I had expanded my awareness out into my fingertips (in fact, I had small hematomas on my fingers the next morning). I had totally expanded to my experience of fear so nothing was left in my body to be solid and dense, nothing left to contract. It was all free fall.

Recovering the Self

Movement therapy is essentially a recognition process, a knowing again or remembering who we are. One of its major purposes is to affirm the experience of being fully alive. The transpersonal approach assumes that one is in the continual act of becoming. As we become aware of how we actually move and relearn that we have arms and toes and genitals, we begin to remember the freedom we originally had to keep discovering ourselves in the world. We remember old feelings and sensations, some pleasant, some most unpleasant, each gradually acknowledged and integrated. Each knowing enriches the mover and the mover's kinetic sense.

The major key to open this process seems to be the recognition of inner signals, the streamings, pressures, tinglings, surges that lie below the surface tension. Most of us avoid that recognition and the confrontation with self that follows, not only by tensing ourselves but also by talking to ourselves continually so that nothing else can be attended to. Maslow called the inner signals "the impulse voices" and observed that in most neuroses the inner signals are weak or have disappeared (to be replaced by the internal dialogue, or with psychotics, whole worlds of voices).[2] "Recovering the self *must*, as a *sine qua non*, include the recovery of the ability to have and to cognize these signals, to know what and whom one likes and dislikes, what is enjoyable and what is not" (p. 33).

Tense persons are often experientially empty persons, for whom others' opinions, a list or schedule, internalized Mom and Dad, make their choices for them. Recognizing the inner impulses, however, can seem dangerous and frightening after long repression. For example, what might one want to do with one's hands if one weren't sitting on them or holding them stiffly at one's sides? And besides, moving around like that is silly, isn't it?

Transpersonal movement therapy challenges the system that maturity is exclusively a process of taking on the appropriate role and doing it well. That sense of maturity looks like rigidification.

Transpersonal movement therapy supports the pulsation of energy within the human form and assists in the risk of becoming *more*. Recognition, and allowing of inner impulse, is the fundamental vocabulary of life with which a person forms his or her relationship to self and to the world.

Authentic Movement

The bridge between inner impulse and form is a way of moving that we can call authentic movement. Authentic movement is more than involvement and spontaneity. It also involves a shift in the use of attention, and that ability to shift and focus free attention gives movement consciousness. The combination of attending while moving carries it beyond habitual repetition and distinguishes it from our functional movement. The quality of attention is based on a special kind of awareness.

This *awareness* of life working within us is something fundamentally different from observing, fixing and comprehending from the outside. In such observing and comprehending he who comprehends stands apart from

---

2. Abraham H. Maslow, *The Farther Reaches of Human Nature* (New York: The Viking Press, 1971).

171

the comprehended and observed. But in becoming *aware*, the experience remains one with the experiencer and transforms him by taking hold of him. Whenever an experience changes a person it happens unnoticed in the greater awareness of what has been experienced. To become aware means to regain the oneness with the original reality of life.[3]

Allowing, an integral aspect of attention, has two dimensions: giving permission to oneself (even if it's silly or scary or confusing) and allowing whatever emerges to be visible. From a point of relaxed, active waiting, we can "mobilize our attention so that the energy can express itself. This attitude would be the *act of attention;* we follow what happens, concentrating on it. The movement leads and the mover follows."[4] (p. 283).

Attentive movement can open the channel for inner experience to find form in space and time. Such movement is always surprising, especially to the mover, who has brought up the unknown from within.

My experience of people who participate in a profound movement therapy process is that they go through repeated, identifiable cycles with many instances of discrete awareness, "little learnings." Individuals will learn, for example, that they have been holding their whole body in a burdened way. Then they will begin to understand that the burden has something to do with their relationship to gravity and needing to "keep on top of it." They will begin to explore their fear of falling and its source. Those little learnings seem to be cumulative, so that at a certain point the movement process itself takes over, if you allow it, with its own quite visible, magnetic laws. If someone in the room engages in authentic movement, it will draw the attention of everyone in the room. It is unmistakable, like an explosion. All those little experiences of awareness come together in a new form.

One client had been involved with those little learnings for several sessions at the time of this particular breakthrough. While moving within the structure of following a sensation in his

---

3. Karlfried Durckheim, *Hara: The Vital Centre of Man* (New York: Samuel Weiser, 1975), p. 159.
4. Mary Whitehouse, "C. G. Jung and Dance Therapy: Two Major Principles," in *Eight Theoretical Approaches in Dance-Movement Therapy*, edited by Penny Lewis Bernstein (Dubuque, Iowa: Kendall-Hunt, 1979), p. 27.

stomach, he found himself catapulted directly into the reexperience of his five-year-old feelings of pain and abandonment about a serious, crippling illness. His cognitive mind had already adjusted quite well to his limitations, his atrophied leg, not being able to run, and so on. His unconscious mind, however, had given previous signals in dreams, moods, recurring daily patterns, that some material was unfinished. In this movement process, he let go into the full intensity of the fear, pain, and helplessness that his five-year-old body had been unable to complete. This experience effortlessly generated several others (some on his own) over the next few weeks, in which he acknowledged, felt, and expressed, both in movement and drawing, his deep feelings from that time. Tremendous energy was released in this process, which he used to move out of a longstanding impasse both personally and professionally.

In the movement process, resistance/stuckness is material to be sensed and moved. I often have people "become" their stuckness to taste its particular quality for them at that time. Any movement in which the mover is awake can transcend "going through the motions." It can enrich even the trained dancer's "response-ability," because it has the capacity for renewal and freshness that come from one's inexhaustible inner life.

Dichotomies and polarities are the stuck places that most often arise from clients in the conflicts they experience in their life situations. Some people are stuck in one polarity (retreating, for example) and have no experience of initiating or wanting. Others swing from one extreme to the other (e.g., good girl, bad girl) with no sense of the middle ground. When one follows the movement instead of controlling it, contrasts tend to synthesize, to become something else, a new possibility, new movement, new life choices.

Transcendence Through Movement

Letting go into the process of authentic movement often leads through personality issues to experiences of transcendence, connection to the self. This transcendence is visible as being moved, rather than willfully, mentally, effortfully directing the body's action. Authentic movement means fully trusting one's body, allowing fusion between one's brain and one's body cells. The fusion creates movement that is totally involved, unpredictable, elegantly economical.

A professional man who had been working in movement therapy for a few months clearly had access to his authentic responses and had begun to work on the essential issues of his life. He kept returning to themes related to having to *do* something, to "get my act together," on the one hand, and a tremendous inner drive toward freedom, on the other hand, which he experienced as "tearing him up inside." He brought in material to sessions, needed little prompting, and usually began moving immediately.

In one session he began by circling "it" (whatever was pushing or pulling at him, represented by a pillow in the middle of the room). Quickly I could see the almost-visible cord that held him as his movement took on the involved, whole-body focus of authenticity. He was clearly stalking, encountering an aspect of himself with full attention that had a timeless quality to it. I have learned not to interrupt this process, for clients are often so involved that the room disappears for that encounter. Any comment or interpretation that I might see a need to make is irrelevant. At that point, then, my presence was important as the anchor, witness, and permission-giver.

As the man moved in response to his ambivalence and finally became "it," his movement changed, taking on a diffuse, halting, hesitant quality. He later described "it" as vague and foggy; he couldn't see clearly through it. He spent the rest of the session exploring "its" demands and his responses, sometimes moving, sometimes talking to "it." I understand this current phase as a ripening for that client. Each time he moves consciously, he remembers more childhood experience, the image from a recent dream, the connection of his bodily sensations, and he learns to become more of who he is.

WINDOW ON A SESSION:

Introduction: Seeing

Since movement is a universal language, anything that occurs from the time the client(s) walks in is potential material. Most of my work is with individuals, and I generally do not move with them. Sessions usually begin with expanding the emergent movement material. I recognize this potential movement in several ways: I look for areas where the client's body is more dense, areas that are unmoving. Any repeated mannerism, such as hand fidgeting or facial tics, can signal a condensed movement metaphor. Areas of the body that work against each other draw my attention, such as the pelvic area moving forward while the chest and shoulders are retreating. I notice whether impulses to move are recognized and course sequentially through the body to expression or whether the person stops this process, as with a yawn that forms a stretch or is held behind tight jaws and shallow breathing.

My attention is focused on the edge of the movement that is about to happen. In the therapy process the client is encouraged to literally be *more,* to take the hesitancy in his or her hands, allowing the whole body to be hesitant, to breathe around the area that feels painful or numb or hard, and to allow that body sensation space to become a form, an expression. When clients allow the potential movement to arise, they experience directly the flow of energy and aliveness. They reclaim the truth of their actual experience and recreate feedback loops that get covered and distorted when somebody else is given authority to govern their internal experience.

Importance of the Therapist's Attitudes

My attitudes and processing of my experience seem to be critical to the flow of the session. One difference between transpersonal movement therapy and dance therapy, which evolved from the medical model, is my assumption that each client already contains everything necessary for his or her perfect evolution. I acknowledge that the door to this cognition involves a lot of work with personality, as personality constructs stand between the client and his or her connection with the life source. My attitude toward the emergence of personality is to understand that it is held in a bigger container, space. Content-free space is where I rest my body and my attention.

I agree with Durckheim that "one must understand from the core of one's being that all forms are brought forth in stillness and when they are fulfilled, taken back again.''[5] My degree of willingness to be present, to go beyond boundaries and roles to touch the actual current of life in clients, to go on their journey with them, modulates the flow of the session and its relative degree of furthering the client's awareness and choice. I support the client's acknowledgment that his or her body is both whole and holy.

If I'm working from a transpersonal perspective, I don't take the personality very seriously. I look for the movement that expresses essence, supporting and reflecting that with my own body attitude and with every level of my experience. I continue to reflect essence no matter what kind of role, drama with spouse, or other element emerges. I still honor that, but I don't take it seriously. I don't act as if that is the only alternative. I know from over a decade of work with people that supporting the emergence of essence supports the perfect next step in the client's process.

Essence and Personality

Essence is what one sees out of the corner of the eye, the underlying rhythm and context of the actual visible movement. If one were humming along to that person's movement, it would be the melody of the tune. It can't be pushed; it can't be structured; it can't be called up on demand.

Personality looks contracted. When "seeing" a person's body, most personality is very gross and so quite visible. The contraction is large. The whole body is bent by it. But the contraction can also be subtle, just the slightest withdrawal from the moment.

In most persons, movement is circulating personality all the time, with only rare moments of essence breaking through. When essence emerges, the movement has that sense of inevitability and enormous vitality. This is a transformative experience, and the transformation can be created in movement, that space where something else takes over.

One particular movement experience with a twenty-six-year-old married woman provides an electrifying example of essence emerging. This overweight, unhappy woman felt profoundly

5. Durckheim, *Hara*, p. 161.

stuck in her body, her marriage, her life. We were actively exploring "stuck" in this session. She used the floor as if it were glue and stuck alternate parts of herself to the floor while continuing to move, illustrating her life stance, as if nothing were amiss. She eventually shifted to her shoulders and recognized that burdened part as the nexus of her stuck feeling. She chose to allow the inner voice in her shoulders to emerge in sound and movement, with the phrases, "I'll show you," "I'll sacrifice, I'll give up, I love to suffer," welling up and out, much to her surprise. Suddenly she began cackling and crouching, darting about the studio like a demon. The hair on my arms stood up as I felt the presence of almost pure hatred. After a few minutes of this frenzied, inferno movement, she seemed to wake up, looked at me, and said, "I always thought I was the 'bad seed.'"

Her early life experiences had been so ugly (incest; alcoholic parents) that she decided a long time ago that she must be evil to cause such misery. As this realization swept over her in the present, she felt the need to open the windows, to put on beautiful music, and to exorcise the palpable presence in the room. This session was the turning point in her learning to love herself.

Through the Window

The actual movement continua and experiences I draw from have simplified over the years. Most important, seemingly, is to know how clients experience the ongoing pull of gravity, how much space they occupy both internally and in interactions, their relationship to the fundamental axes of possibility: rising, sinking, expanding, contracting, and so forth. The structure I generally provide in sessions is to define wide boundaries around the potential material (e.g., an unpleasant stomach sensation) and to encourage clients to begin expanding out into it in their own way.

Clients spend as much time not moving as moving, and they may be lying down, sitting, standing or using all the available space to move through. Sessions rarely look the same, because each client's process is unique. I intend to honor that inner knowing and internal direction by being as transparent myself as possible and by repeatedly returning my attention to the edge of the becoming movement in the client.

An example of expanding a habitual movement might illustrate the interrelationship between my process and that of the client. Suppose the person were fidgeting with the hands, a common pattern. Working with this from a transpersonal approach, I would first feel that process in myself, as the first level of intervention. My fundamental process would be to alternately observe and internally attend, seeing the movement and feeling my responses, watching the quality and allowing it to move me. I would hear the quality of the sounds, as if the movement were a symphony in my head. I would take in information as openly as possible, without labeling it in myself.

At the same time, I would allow another part of myself to be open to any images that might occur to me. Most often I share these images with clients as part of the process we are engaging in together. Frequently it fits some aspect of their experience that I could not have logically predicted. The image-making capacity depends on allowing whatever is coming up to do so. If clients can learn just that, it gives them enormous freedom from the pattern of clinging desperately to their current position until they are wrenched loose and grab for the next available position.

Our bodies are a visual representation of a life stance.

I also perceive the quality of the compromise, the conflict. I'm thinking of one woman I just saw, and I sensed the desperation in her from her hand movement. As it emerged, I allowed that feeling to move its way through me without my impeding its progress. If, as sometimes happens, it reaches a stuck place of mine, I attend to that. This is a process of really participating in the client's process. The willingness of both parties creates the crucible where change happens.

In that session, the woman's composite realization was a surprising sense of how angry she felt and how scared she was to express that feeling directly. It literally leaked out through her fingertips.

Embodying the Concepts

In this culture, unlike others across the world and throughout time, we are not well acquainted with the healing nature of movement itself. We need to know what it is good for, the end product. How can movement, being nonverbal, carry over into verbal communication? How can something you learn about the way you stand change the way you communicate with your spouse?

We must remember that the *way* one stands is not the issue, but, rather, the quality of moving when standing in that particular way, *experiencing* oneself in the moment, is what enables fuller communication to take place. Verbal communication is the end product of the person's willingness to express.

For example, I remember one woman who discovered that she had been habitually standing on her toes for years, but she really hadn't *experienced* standing on her toes. When she actually began standing on her whole foot, both feet, and explored her expression from that root, she realized during the next week a parallel in her relationship with her husband. Before, she had always been anticipating him, his wants, his feelings. She had kept on her toes in relation to him. When she stood solidly on her own feet, it totally changed her communication style with him.

Transformation occurs at a deep level in this style of movement therapy, and it is allowed to reverberate through the whole system. The therapy is based on the assumption that any contracted area (a hyperextended knee, for example) has life stored inside the defense system. Because the knee usually has no sensation, awareness is lacking. The knee is a part of the person that has become mechanical. But if that suspension begins to come alive again, the life that was stored starts flowing again, bringing with it any leftover, unfinished, old movement experiences, contractions that haven't expanded. All of the life of the cell that had been suspended while the knee contracted is going to start flowing through the system again. The end product of that flow may be what in our society is the basic form of communication, speech.

Core Concepts

The embodiment of three core concepts from transpersonal psychology — willingness, space, and unity — can be well illustrated in movement process. Here are some clinical experiences from my practice over the last decade.

Willingness

Since willingness truly seems to be the key, trying to recognize and describe what a willing attitude would look like has been an intriguing study for me. If the client is willing, anything is possible, so it seemed valuable to be able to uncover and encourage that attitude in the concrete arena for learning to love yourself — movement therapy. I began to see over time that willing clients had some commonalities. Their bodies were more toned; their skin lay smoothly connected to their muscles. Their natural movement preferences matched more closely their internal experiences, seemed truer. That congruence doesn't mean that their internal life was necessarily in harmony or satisfying, however. In one case the client's internal life was psychotic. Her face grimaced, her body twisted — but she knew it. The germ of consistency was already present.

In my studies, the movement of willing clients was generally more fluid, though rarely throughout their bodies, which contained the usual hunches, burdens, and numb areas. The quality of the movement itself dealt better with transitions than more resistant clients I've treated. Unwillingness tends to look more static in time and space, as if the person were rooted to the spot. The fluidity of the more willing mover wasn't chaotic or without purpose, though. It rather seemed to follow an inner thread. The form of the movement looked more reed-like than steely. Possibly, part of willingness is the repeated choice to let go, even of the comfortable places. With these clients, the suspicion that no one else was going to rescue them seemed to allow the risk of letting go of life stances and movement styles that no longer fit their sense of responsibility for who they were. Willingness seems to short-circuit the need to understand, the need to figure it out before change can be risked.

One client's work with his lifelong push against a feeling of anger illustrates willingness in action. The man's body looked as if he had a surgical-strength rubber band attached to his chin and his genitals, so that whenever he stood to his full height, he experienced vaguely a sexual threat and excitation.

This forty-year-old man's back was a reservoir of old burdens and resentments, and his shoulders were especially hunched and thick, painful. All this conflict was upheld quite tentatively on tense thighs, locked knees, and curled-under toes, making walking itself fatiguing.

Most of the movement work with this client has begun by acknowledging the most prominent body sensation, which he then amplifies, exploring throughout his body (chasing it around), breathing around, and following. He uses movement as a form of meditation; when the analyst part of his mind becomes active, he gently turns his attention back to the actual sensations, especially the vague, fleeting ones. The words that generally emerge some time in the sequence are, "I don't know," followed by a larger exhalation of relief and the formation of a definite movement expression of that vague body sensation. For example, one energetic flinging-off movement emerged out of his stomach uneasiness.

His willingness seems contingent on his acknowledging that his body is a whole system with its own intrinsic relationships and laws, not necessarily dominated by his cognitive brain. Each experiencing and expressing cycle has enlarged his aliveness, his choices in his everyday life, his capacity for renewal. He currently strides more easily, has thrown off the burdens, and sees more clearly into himself and others.

Space

Individuals' relationship to space is critical to their sense of belonging in the world and represents their method of grounding or security. How much space people use in their movement and how much internal space they are aware of parallels their cycle of expansion and contraction. I often have clients move in that particular structure in the first sessions, expanding until they feel as far out as they wish to go, then contracting as far in as feels right, and again expanding. Most people use very little of their potential space, and their feelings about security, protection, and guardedness emerge with this focus of exploration. Birth issues especially are triggered by the experience of expanding right to the edge of possibility, into asymmetry and fears of falling.

Use of space also indicates degree of self-esteem. One older woman who had ovarian cancer moved through space as if she were constantly testing the water. It emerged that at home in her small kitchen with her husband, who was a huge block, a retired military man, she repeatedly made herself smaller whenever they had to cross paths. Her inner experience of herself was a mix of unfinished little-girl needs to skip and frolic and turn and the acculturated constrictions her body had accumulated from years of having her desires blocked while her responsibilities to others were accented. The choice to make oneself smaller is a giving up that breeds resentment, confusion, and eventually hopelessness.

Internal space, the sense of being at home in one's body, is a primary goal of movement therapy. A woman with many self-image issues was working with falling into pillows and noticing the stiff, dead-wood feelings in her arms, whereupon she remembered a childhood incident of falling off a swing set. She had expected her arms to break her fall, and remembered the fear paralysis they locked into, as well as her decision to "disown" them for being so stupid as to allow her to badly hurt herself. From that point, she apparently had contracted severely at her shoulder joints, so that her arms hung loosely and fairly ineffectively at her sides. The process of owning her arms again involved a long movement dialogue between her arms and the rest of her, reclaiming reaching, throwing, pushing, and swinging — all the movement that arms do.

Use of space in interrelationships is largely learned, as are role behaviors. A young man was exploring "sideways" movement one afternoon when he began to feel prickly along his back and seemed to need to crouch and guard himself. He looked as if he were being held, so I asked him to imagine a tether attached to him and someone or something at the other end. The someone became his father, who stood behind him and prevented him from moving forward. The young man then recalled a complex series of memories of all the ways he had felt tethered in his lack of free time —the constant demands of his father in the family store, the absence of acknowledgment of his desires, and so on. From that point, he could begin to reclaim that widening space, and his body (especially the chest) began to fill out as he presented himself in the world as more capable and free.

Unity

The illusion of separation is most visible in the body fragmentation and movement dissonance of conflict. As long as one holds someone else responsible or to blame, experiences of unity are rare. Fears of being consumed and annihilated, dissolving — all those birth-related issues — block the free flow of awareness out into space and unity. My attitude in work is that we are exploring the obstacles between the client's present life and his or her full potential. An obstacle is like a logjam in the flow, and actively loving the obstacle frees the jam. I feel the obstacle in myself and love it, move with it. I see the obstacle in the client and love it, move with it.

Most often in sessions the experience of unity is the end result of letting go of a particular pattern of moving through the world. The exhilarating freedom of dropping an old resentment lodged between the shoulder blades, or straddling more of the ground when walking, or standing and facing a fearful situation that used to induce averted eyes and clenched stomach are the moments of free attention, the moments of full breath and oneness with life.

The experience of unity seems to always be available behind the veil of projection. In a women's movement therapy group we spent one session exploring literally moving behind veils, as is commonplace in much of the Moslem world. The women used large pieces of cloth to drape themselves and began exploring space and the rhythms of covering and uncovering. They worked a long time individually, then in pairs, and finally in a spontaneous swaying circle dance under a parachute. The video I made of the group clearly reflected the phrases of taking on roles — the harem girl, the nun, the aloof matron, the invisible slave — and the tentative and then more abandoned release of those roles. The momentum of covering and uncovering built as group members began using their cloths in elaborate coverings and uncoverings of each other, learning to include another in that universal rhythm. At an inspired moment I put "Scheherazade" on the record player, and the movement became even more circular and inclusive. As the covered form of the women swayed quietly, the presence of unity was radiantly evident.

MOVEMENT EXPERIMENTS

Each of the following activities is designed to illustrate a particular facet of transpersonal approaches in therapy. These are based on the experience that is possible when one lets go of content and focuses on process.

Experiment 1

This experiment is to be done with a partner. Ideally, choose a time when you've put aside schedules and demands; use an open space where you feel comfortable; and have nonrhythmic music in the background (Brian Eno's "Ambient" series is especially good for this purpose).

1. Have the partners (you could be one) stand facing each other, each person with one foot about a half-stride behind the front leg. They are to experiment with rocking their weight from front to back and make any adjustments that allow them to feel more fluid, as if the hip, knee, and ankle joints were on rollers.
2. Have partner A offer his or her forearm to partner B, allowing every other body part to relax. Partner B is to place his or her fingertips on partner A's forearm, with pressure somewhere between feather-light (withheld) and anchor-heavy (giving up responsibility).
3. Ask partner B to close his or her eyes, while partner A begins to move his or her arm smoothly, slowly, and in random patterns in space. The objective for partner B is to maintain the same extent of finger contact throughout, and for partner A to consciously make his or her movement wavelike. They will notice how much information is transmitted through the fingertips. Each time partner B anticipates or tenses, partner A will feel it. Exhaling completely assists in releasing tension, for both partners.
4. After several minutes, have the two switch roles, then take time to share their actual experience.

This experiment ages well. With practice, participants report experiences of unity, not only with their partner but with life energy. Images of rivers, floating feelings, enlivening of unnoticed body parts, and the positive experience of giving over control to another person have also transpired for participants.

Experiment 2

This experiment can be done individually or in partnership. To simplify the activity at the beginning, use a partner as observer until the observer in oneself is developed. This structure can be used as a tool for discovering automatic responses and enlivening them.

1. The initial framework for this experience is relatively unstructured. Simply have the mover allow and follow movement impulses as they emerge in his or her body. This movement can be done lying down, sitting, or standing, and may involve large movement or small gestures of hands and feet. Movements can not be *right* or *wrong* — just that which wants to be moved.

2. Let this random moving continue for some time, even if the person runs out of things to do and starts repeating previous movements. Meanwhile, the observer (either the partner or your mind's eye) is to notice the movement to which the mover keeps returning. This may be a discrete gesture that is repeated; a way of moving from place to place, such as in short, quick bursts; or a quality or style, such as circular arm movements or a tunnel-like focus of the torso. The important aspect to notice is the repetition.

3. Let the attention focus on this identified movement now, by having the person repeat it, taking some time with each of the following variations:

   a. Make the movement larger in the sense of *more* of whatever it is. Exaggerate it beyond "everyday" dimensions and really bring it into relief. Let the whole body become that quality. Initially, this may feel ridiculous or silly; allow that feeling and whatever other responses arise to be part of the experience.

b. Take the kernel of the movement, the quality, and do its opposite. For example, if the movement involved arm circles, have the arms make only angular, straight lines in space. Notice the body's response to trying this opposite.

c. Take the movement and let another part of your body move it. For example, do the arm circles and let the hips move in the same way.

d. Let the movement alternate between exaggerating the identified pattern, moving its opposite, exaggerating, opposing, many times. Notice the tendency of qualities to blend, to find a new kind of movement somewhere between the two.

4. Allow a few moments of reflection time for the participant to ask:

a. How am I creating this pattern in my daily life?

b. Is this movement familiar, like any other experience I've had?

c. What have I discovered about the way I think I should move and be in the world, and how do I feel when I change that habitual response?

Experiment 3

Remember the little wooden, multi-jointed animals or dolls, about three-four inches high, on a round stand with a button on the bottom? Push the button, and the doll collapses; let go, and it springs back up. This experiment is based on that principle and is an active way to learn the art of "going with" while remaining grounded. It is fun to do in a group with partners, to experience the differences in everyone's style of resistance and flow.

1. For contrast, have partner A take a position (both feet on the floor) where the person feels he or she can't be moved. Have partner B circle partner A's body until partner B can see the "loophole," the flat place, the area which, if nudged just slightly, causes a loss of balance.

Switch roles, perhaps a few times with various positions, to have the participants really experience the body sense of "taking a position," and to experience its relative security.

2. Have partner A take a fairly wide stance, knees slightly bent, eyes closed, exhaling each breath fully. Have partner B use his or her hand to push various parts of the partner's body lightly: shoulders, head, hip, stomach, thigh, etc. Ask partner A to imagine his or her body as a spiralling form, allowing each push to move through the body, going with it along the spiral until the energy of the push dissolves, then returning to the central position. This is to be repeated with the next push, and so on. After about five minutes, the partners' roles should be reversed.

3. Everyone seems to have a central tension reservoir, the place that responds reflexively to a push by becoming rigid. It could be one's lower back, chest, back of the neck. Have partner A nudge partner B at these various body places. Partner B will have the experience of rigidifying, losing balance, rigidifying, losing balance, perhaps many times before deciding to let go of the automatic response and explore the sensation of "going with." Reverse roles, and be sure to take time to share discoveries with the partner and the group.

Bibliography

Andresen, Gail, and Weinhold, Barry. *Connective Bargaining: Communicating About Sex.* Englewood Cliffs, NJ: Prentice-Hall, 1981.

Bach, Richard. *Illusions: The Adventures of a Reluctant Messiah.* New York: Delacorte, 1977.

Bandler, Richard, and Grinder, John. *Frogs Into Princes: Neuro Linguistic Programming.* Moab, UT: Real People Press, 1979.

Benoit, Hubert. *The Supreme Doctrine.* New York: Harper, 1960.

Capra, Fritjof. *The Tao Of Physics.* Berkeley: Shombala, 1975.

Ethinger, Edward F. *Ego And Archetype.* Baltimore, MD: Penguin, 1972.

Evans-Wentz, W. Y. *Tibetan Book Of The Dead.* New York: Oxford University Press, 1960.

Feild, Reshad. *The Last Barrier: A Journey Through The World Of Sufi Teaching.* New York: Harper & Row, 1976.

Feild, Reshad. *The Invisible Way: A Love Story For The New Age.* New York: Harper & Row, 1979.

Fordham, Michael. *New Developments In Analytical Psychology.* London: Routledge & Kegan Paul, 1957.

Golas, Thaddeus. *The Lazy Man's Guide To Enlightenment.* Palo Alto, CA: Seed Center, 1974.

Goldstein, Joseph. *The Experience Of Insight.* Santa Cruz, CA: Unity Press, 1975.

Grof, Stanislov. *Realms Of The Human Unconscious.* New York: Viking, 1974.

Gunther, Bernard. *Energy Ecstasy And Your Seven Vital Chakras.* Los Angeles: Guild of Tutors Press, 1978.

Hendricks, Gay. "What do I do after they tell me how they feel?" *Personnel & Guidance Journal,* January, 1977.

Hendricks, Gay. *Learning To Love Yourself.* Englewood Cliffs, NJ: Prentice-Hall, in press.

Hendricks, Gay, and Leavenworth, Carol. *How To Love Every Minute Of Your Life.* Englewood Cliffs, NJ: Prentice-Hall, 1978.

Hoffman, Robert. *Getting Divorced From Mother and Dad.* New York: E. P. Dutton & Co., 1976.

Joy, W. Brugh. *Joy's Way: A Map For The Transformational Journal.* Los Angeles: J. P. Tarcher, 1979.

Kaplan, Louise. *Oneness And Separateness: From Infant To Individual.* New York: Simon and Schuster, 1978.

Klaus, Marshall, and Kennell, John. *Maternal-Infant Bonding.* St. Louis, MO: C. V. Mosby Company, 1976.

Kopp, Sheldon. *An End To Innocence: Facing Life Without Illusions.* New York: Bantam Books, 1981.

Krishnamurti, J. *The Awakening Of Intelligence.* New York: Harper and Row, 1974.

LeBoyer, Frederick. *Birth Without Violence.* New York: Knopf, 1975.

Loevinger, Jane. *Ego Development.* San Francisco: Jossey-Bass, 1976.

Orr, Leonard, and Ray, Sondra. *Rebirthing In The New Age.* Millbrae, CA: Celestial Arts, 1977.

Maslow, Abraham H. *The Farther Reaches Of Human Nature.* New York: Viking Press, 1971.

Pearce, Joseph Chilton. *The Magical Child: Rediscovering Nature's Plan For Our Children.* New York: E. P. Dutton, 1977.

Ray, Sondra. *Loving Relationships.* Millbrae, CA: Celestial Arts, 1980.

Read, Herbert; Fordham, Michael; and Adler, Gehard, eds. *The Collected Works of C. G. Jung: Vol. 9, Archetypes and the Collective Unconscious.* New York: Pantheon Books, 1953, pp. 1-147.

Weinhold, Barry. "Metaphysical Approaches to Helping." *Elementary School Guidance and Counseling* 14, no. 2, December, 1979.

Weinhold, Barry, and Andresen, Gail. *Threads: Unraveling The Mysteries Of Adult Life.* New York: Richard Marek Publishers, 1979.

Weinhold, Barry, and Elliott, Lynn. *Transpersonal Communication*. Englewood Cliffs, NJ: Prentice-Hall, 1979.

Weinhold, Barry K., and Hendricks, Gaylord. "Transpersonal Approaches to Counseling and Psychotherapy." *Counseling and Human Development* 12, no. 5 (1980): pp. 1-16.

Wilber, Ken. *No Boundary*. Los Angeles: Center Publications, 1979.

Wilber, Ken. *The Atman Project: A Transpersonal View Of Human Development*. Wheaton, IL: Theosophical Publishing House, 1980.

Appendix

TRANSPERSONAL ORGANIZATIONS

Many networks of people are interested in transpersonal domains. One of the most prominent is the Association for Transpersonal Psychology, P.O. Box 3049, Stanford, CA, 94305. In existence since the late 1960s, ATP publishes the *Journal of Transpersonal Psychology* and sponsors an annual meeting, held usually in summer at Asilomar Conference Center, Monterey, California. ATP also offers other publications and events of interest to transpersonally-oriented individuals.

An International Transpersonal Association has been formed, directed by Stanislav Grof and others, which has sponsored international conferences on several continents. This group can be contacted by writing ITA, Big Sur, California.

The American Psychological Association has a transpersonal interest group that is gathering momentum toward a transpersonal division within APA. In addition, the Association for Humanistic Psychology has many members who are active in transpersonal explorations.

The authors have done many workshops and presentations sponsored by counseling organizations such as the American Personnel and Guidance Association and state affiliates. Interest in transpersonal approaches appears brisk among school counselors and mental health professionals, and most professional organizations that serve them have informal or formal interest groups exploring transpersonal ideas and issues.

RECOMMENDED REBIRTHERS*————————————

Rima Beth
6809 Daugherty
Austin, TX 78757

Mallie Burzon
310 W. 106th St. #4B
New York, NY 10025

Bill Chappelle
111 Oceano Ave.
Santa Barbara, CA 93109

Jody Dubois
2917 - 124th Pl. N.E.
Bellevue, WA 98005

Diane Hinterman
General Delivery
Ross, CA 94957

Steven and Trina Kamp
546 N. Miller
Mesa, AZ 85203

Phil Laut
301 Lyon St.
San Francisco, CA 94117

Fred Lehrman
P.O. Box 7471
San Diego, CA 92107

Bob Mandel
310 W. 106th St. #4B
New York, NY 10025

Jim Morningstar
2728 Prospect Ave.
Milwaukee, WI 53211

Sondra Ray
c/o Universal Seminars
18455 Burbank Blvd., Suite 409
Tarzana, CA 91356

Jack Szumel
656 Bayview Dr.
Aptos, CA 95003

---

*For a complete listing of Rebirthers, see the *Theta International Directory of Rebirthers*, available from: Rima Beth, Director, P.O. Box 10205, Austin, TX 78757.

RECOMMENDED REBIRTHING — THETA TRAINING CENTERS _____

Breath Of Life
Bill Thompson
2601 Parkway No. 454
Philadelphia, PA 19130

Campbell Hot Springs
Yvonne Moriarty
  and Leah Dell Dick
P.O. Box 194
Sierraville, CA 96126

Center for Holistic Psychology
  and Education
Stephen Johnson, Ph.D.
Linda Thistle, Ph.D.
Fran Middleton Johnson
9012 Burton Way
Beverly Hills, CA 90211

Steven and Trina Kamp
546 N. Miller
Mesa, AZ 85282

Life Organization Game
Patricia and David Durovy
2437 N. Booth St.
Milwaukee, WI 53212

Sherrill Lightheart
  and Bill Stallings
1833 N.E. 52 No. 3
Portland, OR 97213

One Year Seminar
Jody Dubois
  and Michael Thompkins
2917 - 124th Pl., N.E.
Bellevue, WA 98005

One Year Seminar
Chiara Eash
Box 492
Lahaska, PA 18931

One Year Seminar
Beverly Smith
5828 Hobart St.
Pittsburgh, PA 15217

Only Miracles, Northeast
  Rebirthers Association
Mallie Burzon and Bob Mandel
310 W. 106th St., #4B
New York, NY 10025

Theta Chicago
Kip and Yvonne Hillman
1870 N. Burling
Chicago, IL 60614

Theta Ganges
Jeffrey Godine
  and Tree Jackson
Box 871
Ganges, British Columbia,
  Canada UOS 1E0

Theta Montreal
Norman Arseneault
  and Micheline Charron
3950 Van Home
Montreal, Canada H3S 1S1

Theta San Francisco
Peter Kane
301 Lyon St.
San Francisco, CA 94117

Theta Texas
Rima Beth
  and Steve Schweigert
6809 Daugherty
Austin, TX 78758

Theta Wisconsin
Jim and Joan Morningstar
2728 N. Prospect
Milwaukee, WI 52311

Threshold
C. W. Light
Usha Sunshine
RR 1, Box 855
Haiku, Maui, Hawaii 96708

Jim Worsley
10802 Margate Rd.
Silver Spring, MD 20901

BASIC GUIDELINES FOR COMMUNICATION _____

1. Say "I" when you are expressing something that you think or feel or have done instead of using words like "you," "they," "people," etc. Thus, you acknowledge that what you are saying is about you, and thereby let people get to know you.

2. Avoid asking questions unless you really need information or need to know something. Often, questions are an indirect way of making statements and a way to shift responsibility onto someone else. For example, "Don't you think that . . .?" is a sneaky way of making a statement without taking responsibility for it.

3. Avoid discounting, which is acting as if what *you* think or feel is more important than what the other person thinks and feels, or denigrating yourself and acting as if the other person is more important than you are. Some examples of discounting are:

   a. interrupting (discounting the person talking).

   b. not speaking because you think you'll sound stupid (self-discounting).

   c. not taking the other person's desires into account; e.g., deciding what you will do on a date (discounting the other person).

   d. saying things that put yourself down (self-discounting). The opposite of discounting is accounting — taking you, your feelings, thoughts, and desires into account, along with the other person.

4. Don't rescue — which is doing for someone what he or she can do for him/herself. This is discounting the other person because you are acting as if he or she can't take care of him/herself.

5. Avoid interpreting. An interpretation is when you tell someone what motivates them, why they feel or think or act the way they do; for example, "You are an angry person." The

main reason this is not a very good way to communicate is that the other person will probably feel defensive. (Example: "You're a defensive person.")

Instead, tell the person how you feel or what you *think*; make your statement from an "I" position ("I think . . .") or describe what makes you think as you do. (Example: "I notice that you argue and disagree with most of the things I say, and it's hard for me to talk to you.")

6. Feelings and thoughts are two different things, although we often confuse them in language. For instance, "I feel that you are wrong about that" is actually a thought, not a feeling. Use "I feel . . ." only when expressing feelings (anger, sadness, fear, happiness, fatigue, etc.).

7. Avoid using exaggerations or exaggerated words such as "always," "never," "incredible," "the most . . . in the world," etc. This is often a way of justifying your ineffectiveness, avoiding a problem, or avoiding responsibility for your behavior. For example: "I was so angry, I couldn't help myself." The fact is that you *could* help yourself.

8. Avoid qualifying statements or phrases such as "perhaps," "maybe," "I guess," unless you *really* are unsure. Such words are often a way of avoiding responsibility for what you say. Likewise, the word "try" is often used as a way of really saying, "I won't do it." Trying is very different from *doing*.

9. Avoid such statements as "I can't" and "I have to" unless that is really the case. Rarely are we actually unable or incapable of doing something, and rarely do we "have to" do anything, unless someone is physically forcing us. Actually, we choose to behave the way we do in most cases, often because if we did not we would suffer unpleasant consequences.

10. Confront other people's misstatements. Confrontation is a sign of caring. When you ignore or go along with someone's game-playing, discounting, and so on, you are actually hurting that person and acting as if you don't care. You can

confront in a caring way without attacking the person or his or her behavior.

11. Take responsibility for how you feel, think, and behave. Don't say "You made me angry," because that makes your feelings someone else's responsibility. Instead say, "I am angry because . . ." (stating your reasons). Avoid saying "make(s) me feel."